YOUR BLACK FRIEND HAS SOMETHING TO SAY

A Memoir in Essays

Melva Graham

Pact Press

Published by Pact Press
An imprint of
Regal House Publishing, LLC
Raleigh, NC 27612
All rights reserved

https://pactpress.com

Printed in the United States of America

ISBN -13 (paperback): 9781646030187
ISBN -13 (epub): 9781646030453
Library of Congress Control Number: 2019952294

Interior and cover design by Lafayette & Greene
lafayetteandgreene.com
Cover images © by musicman/Shutterstock
Author image courtesy of @PhotosbyJamaal

Regal House Publishing, LLC
https://regalhousepublishing.com

Printed in the United States of America

"For Good" from the Broadway musical *Wicked*
Music and Lyrics by Stephen Schwartz
Copyright © 2003 Stephen Schwartz
All rights reserved. Used by permission of Grey Dog Music (ASCAP).

For Mom and Dad

Contents

AUTHOR'S NOTE

This book is not about you. It's about my experience of you—which is to say, it's about me. That being said, I changed your name. I changed everyone's name—except my own. I also changed the name of a few places. Just in case. You're welcome.

INTRODUCTION

They're called "microaggressions"—and they're a macro pain in the ass. They're underhanded, race-related remarks that undermine who I am as a black woman, reinforce a racial hierarchy, and reveal an unconscious but blatant bias. They're subtle and skillfully done. They're like a sociological sickness—particularly in the suburbs. I remember how relieved I was when I found out there was an actual name for them. Here I thought people were just being assholes.

I've got a lot of racial baggage.

Can you tell?

I'm like a hoarder. I've held on to every racially charged moment in my life since I was six years old. My mind is like a microaggression museum. On the left is the time I posed for a picture between two white women and one shouted, "Look, reverse Oreo!" On the right is the time my coworker brought her dog into work and nicknamed it Nigga. Up ahead, you'll hear the voice of a small child I used to babysit telling me I have to do what he tells me to do, because I'm his slave. In the gift shop I sell T-shirts and mugs that say, "You talk white," and postcards that say, "Pretty for a black girl." Even the most pernicious of pieces is semiprecious in that it shaped so much of who I am today—and I'm not altogether thrilled with who I am today. I let things slide. And I let people off the hook. And I look the other way. I'm like an enabler for white privilege.

If you have something racist to say, I'm the one to say it to. If you want to touch black hair, I'm the one to ask. If you want to make a generalization about my community—a community you know nothing about—I'm the one to make

3

it to. Silence is so ingrained in me it has become instinctive. I'll walk away wounded but without saying a word. I might even force a small smile to my face to let you know things are still cool between us.

I've always looked out for the emotional well-being of white people. It's a skill set I'm so well accomplished in, I've actually been paid to do it. I'm a nanny. The help. I take care of rich white kids and their rich white parents. At times, it's like I'm babysitting the kids I went to school with. I'm now their nanny. I'm an actress, too, but the only acting I get to do, really, is as a nanny. When microaggressions occur, as they so often do, I get to act like I'm not offended, like I'm not hurt, when really I am.

The underlying message in all this is that I, as a black woman, should sit down, shut up, and stay home. This message has metastasized deep within my marrow. I receive this message when a black woman is sentenced to twenty years in prison for standing her ground, firing a warning shot, defending herself against an abusive husband. I receive this message when a black woman is pulled over for failing to use her turn signal, is arrested, and then dies in police custody. I receive this message when a black woman is gunned down after knocking on a stranger's door for help. I receive this message in movies where black women are barely visible. I receive this message in the media where our voices are drowned out and dismissed.

But a shift is happening…a movement is taking place…a revolution has started…*Black Girls Rock*…*Black Girl Magic*…*Black Girl Dangerous*. Black women are stepping into themselves and taking back the power that was always theirs, but instead of *receiving* the message, we're writing our own. Suddenly I'm being asked to show up, stand up, and speak up…but I don't know how. It wasn't part of my programming.

Culturally speaking, my identity, my blackness, is caught between two generations of hyper-visibility: the past Civil Rights Movement and the present Civil Rights Movement. I grew up in between the two, in the 80s and 90s, the age of cultural assimilation and upward mobility for blacks—well, some blacks. Race and racism were still ongoing issues for the black community, of course, but blackness, as an identity, was rarely seen or heard—at least not by me. It wasn't part of the national conversation. The new narrative was we're all the same. We're all equal. We don't see color. We don't see race. The Black Power and Black Pride Movements went from a rousing chorus to a faint whisper. In 1968 we sang "Say It Loud—I'm Black and I'm Proud." In 1982 we sang "Ebony and Ivory." See the difference? One is hyper-visible. One is invisible. This was my generation. The "There Can Be Only One" generation. The "Can't We All Just Get Along" generation. I want in on today's generation. I want in on the "Black Lives Matter Marching In the Streets" generation. The "No Justice, No Peace" generation. The "Kneeling During the National Anthem" generation. If there were messages from the black community to black youth counter to the ones I received as a child, then I missed out on them. They were lost on me. I wasn't told to "Fight the Power" or "Do the Right Thing." I was told to sit quietly and wait to be called on. What I realize, though, is that as a black woman, nobody is going to call on me, because no one wants to hear what I have to say. What I have to say is not pleasant and it's not polite and it shakes up the status quo. It's my job to show up, stand up, and speak up anyway—but frankly, I'm not sure if I'm up to it.

Nothing I have to say is newsworthy. I haven't lost loved ones to police brutality. I haven't been racially profiled. I haven't been stopped and frisked. You won't find any of my stories scrolling at the bottom of the screen of a cable news show. "Breaking news...intoxicated white male calls black female Hot Chocolate after Santana concert tonight in Pittsburgh." The NAACP will not advocate for me. Al Sharpton will more than likely sit this one out.

Still, I have something to say.

There is a narrative about the black community that is constantly pushed and published in white America, one I don't identify with. I'm writing not so much to change the narrative but to contribute to it, to make it as varied and layered and diverse as the people it speaks for.

My name is Melva.

You may know me as the only black person in the room.

I wasn't born in the segregated South, and my grand-mother didn't raise me. I grew up in a two-parent home in a suburb outside of Pittsburgh. My parents have been married over forty-five years. They took me back-to-school shopping when I was a kid and sent me care packages in college. I didn't march with King or participate in sit-ins at diners that refused to serve me. I spent my summers learning how to swim at the YMCA, playing Nintendo with my sister, running lemonade stands with friends, singing and dancing at theater camp, and taking classes to prepare for the SATs. I never rode at the back of the bus; the back of the bus is where all the cool kids sat on the way to school or on field trips, and I was never considered cool. I'm diversity—the All-American Black Girl (if that's even a thing), best friend of the All-American White Girl Next Door. I'm Dionne from *Clueless*. I'm Lisa from *Saved By The Bell*. I'm what's-her-name from *Troop Beverly Hills*. I'm Tootie from *The* Fucking *Facts of Life*.

My idea of struggle is breaking the box society has put me in...showing up for myself, as myself, and, more often than not, by myself in a country that continues to discourage me from doing so...and carving out my own experience as a woman of color, an experience I can own and champion as valid, legit, and indisputably Black.

PART ONE

READING RAINBOW

It's 1988. I'm the only black kid in my first grade class. My best friend, Renee, is in the room across the hall, and Humphrey, the only black boy in the grade, is in the room next to hers. There are three black kids, and three first grade classes, and each of us is put into one. This is what diversity looks like.

Renee and I were fast friends. She was short and slim with bushy brown hair and a complexion that matched mine. We shared snacks and traded stickers from our sticker book collection. We celebrated our friendship by exchanging handmade gifts—a friendship bracelet, painted rocks, or a botched birdhouse (that neither of us will use) made from Popsicle sticks.

And then there was Humphrey. He and I were friendly but we weren't friends. Kids made fun of his name and I resisted the urge to laugh. Outside of school, our families went on outings. We'd host lunches and have playdates. Our moms shared stories while we played games, but in school we kept our distance and acted like the other was the new kid.

Meredith was my closest friend in class, but her best friend was Bethany, a petite girl with short blonde hair and cheeks the likes of Alvin, Simon, and Theodore. She and Meredith were inseparable the same way Renee and I were. Bethany looked like she could be Meredith's younger sister the same way Renee looked like she could be mine. The two of them matched.

In reading circle we went around one by one reading a story out loud line by line. It was easy to tell who the strong readers were and who needed to be taken back to kindergarten. I always felt bad for the kid who lost his or her place in the story or struggled to sound out words, looking for help from the child to his left or her right. It was embarrassing for everyone. I had nothing to fear, however. I was the one who gave assistance; I did not require it.

I took a seat in the circle next to Meredith. I was to her left, and Bethany sat in a chair to her right. Bethany's eyes landed on me.

"Meredith!" she said. "What are you doing?" Her eyes darted back and forth between us. "You're sitting next to a black person!"

The world stopped and all eyes were on me.

I'm supposed to do something...I'm supposed to say something... only I have no idea what that thing is...

"So what?" Meredith asked. I didn't know if it was defiance in her voice, or a genuine plea for understanding. She looked confused and affronted. Like she'd been scolded for some careless wrongdoing. She might have been running down the hall, or cutting in line.

Now it was Bethany's turn to look confused and affronted. It seemed sitting next to a black person was something you should know not to do, like talking to strangers, or crossing the street before looking both ways. Perhaps she thought she was doing her friend a favor—expecting her to jump up, brush herself off, and switch seats immediately—and in return, she would confirm Bethany's suspicions, whatever they might be, as true. When she did not, however, Bethany looked displeased and disappointed.

I felt as if I had been placed beneath a heat lamp. A bright and blinding light was shining down on me as I struggled to keep my place in the story. Whether my teacher, Mrs. Campbell, heard the comment, or pretended not to, I don't know, but reading circle went on as planned that afternoon.

If Renee or Humphrey had been sitting in the circle with me I might have met their eyes. They, too, would have heard what was said, and I would have seen my feeling of shock and shame reflected back at me and known I wasn't alone. But Renee was in the room across the hall, and Humphrey was in the room next to hers, and I was by myself. So I stayed silent and stared at my feet.

Before I started Sewickley Academy I attended preschool at Rhema Christian School. One day I came home from school and hid underneath the dining room table without saying a word to anyone. Mom bent down and poked her head under the table and asked me what was wrong. I shrugged my shoulders. Somehow she got me out from under the table and on her lap on the couch where I finally gave in—my teacher had given me a spanking.

Mom marched into school with me the next day, went straight up to my teacher, and had a nice long talk with her in the corner of the room. A few minutes later my teacher came up to me and apologized. I used to wonder, and sometimes still do, would she have spanked me if I had been white? I had never seen her do that to any of the other kids. The ones who looked like they could have been her nieces and nephews, her sons and daughters. It wasn't necessary for any one of them to get a spanking. Why had it been necessary for me? What was it about me that was so bad? My behavior? Or my blackness? When I think about it today it's the shame that saddens me. That it was so great I had to hide from it, hide myself. It seems too much for one so small.

When I came home from school that day after reading circle I didn't hide, not under the dining room table, nor anywhere else. Instead, I told Mom. She stopped what she was doing, pulled out the school directory, picked up the phone, and started dialing.... *I'm getting someone in trouble...I'm getting someone into so much trouble....*

I sat down at the kitchen table with Dad and my sister and waited for Mom to get off the phone with Bethany's mom.

My humiliation and hurt hadn't gone away, and in truth, I don't know if it ever has. It was the first time I had been confronted with race. I knew the color of my skin meant something, but I also knew it wasn't supposed to mean anything. Why was color so confusing? And how did Bethany know to use it against me? And why?

Mom joined me and the rest of the family several minutes later and adopted a voice unlike her own. Even at such a young age, I could detect the sarcasm. "Bethany's mom is *very* sorry," she said, a skeptical expression on her face. "Their family was having a *conversation* about race and Bethany *misunderstood*." Mom returned to her usual voice. "Hmph," she said, "I think she understood just fine."

It seemed Mom had called Mrs. Campbell, too, because she addressed the issue the next day in class. I can no longer remember her words, only the nature of them. Each and every one of us is different. We come in different shapes, sizes, and colors, and when these differences stand together we see just how beautiful we all are, like a bright and beaming rainbow.

When she finished speaking she dismissed the class for recess. She held Bethany and me behind to have a few more words with the two of us. Again, I don't remember what was said. I think I was too uncomfortable to take in anything else. What I do remember was the rest of the class huddled outside the door. I remember everyone gathering around Bethany in the hallway, after the three of us had had our talk, to find out what had happened, what was said, and who was in trouble—Bethany for saying I was black, or me for being black?

I felt like something was wrong with me, as if I was infected with a deadly virus and there was risk of contaminating everyone around me. I remember everyone following Bethany down the hall and out the doors while I was left lagging behind. No one came to me. No one wanted to hear from me. Not even Meredith. They wanted to hear from Bethany. That's who they identified with. Bethany. Not me. I thought I was well liked in class, but suddenly I felt very different.

As the rest of the class drifted onto the field and eventually dispersed, I climbed to the top of Timbertown, a massive wooden structure with bridges and tunnels, and sat alone waiting for the other two classes to be dismissed, waiting for Renee, or perhaps even Humphrey.

I see my six-year-old self, sitting at the top of Timbertown, and I want to join her, to keep her company. I want to offer her some fuzzy animal stickers and an orange Squeeze-It to help take her mind off things, but I can't. And I doubt it would make much difference if I could. I had been introduced to hate, and hate is hard to hold. Still, I'd like to try. I'd like to tell her she's not alone and that being black doesn't mean you don't belong.

I think in some ways what happened to me in first grade stunted my growth. I'm still the same six-year-old who sat in reading circle—head low, eyes cast down, silent, still, perfect penmanship. Today, when someone singles me out for the color of my skin, it is that version of me who emerges. And, in truth, I'm not very kind to her when she does. I don't offer her the care and comfort she needs. I bully her, hoping she'll be better. I ignore her, hoping she'll go away, hoping a bolder, braver girl—woman—will take her place. But that bolder, braver woman is still a girl, shy and unsure of herself, and the distance between her and the woman I want to be has never been greater. The same old thoughts still run through my mind: *I'm supposed to do something...I'm supposed to say something...only I have no idea what that thing is.*

I remember watching a made-for-TV movie with Mom

and Grandma when I was a child. A racial slur was used in the movie, and Grandma turned to me and said, "Melva, if anyone ever calls you that, you better call them a—"

"Nothing!" Mom interjected, talking over Grandma at once.

"A what?" I asked, missing Grandma's last word.

"Nothing!" Mom said again.

"Grandma, what did you say?"

Grandma opened her mouth to speak.

"Ma, stop!" said Mom.

"Grandma, what do I call them?" I asked again.

"You call them nothing, Melva," Mom said. "You come and tell me."

And so that's what I did.

But today, I can't do that. I can't have Mom take care of it the way she did when I was six, although I know she would if I asked her to. I can't hide under the dining room table. I have to fight my own battles. And that's a hard thing to do. Because I'm never just answering back to one person. I'm answering back to a system that was designed to silence me, to shame me, and make me feel small, a system four hundred years in the making.

THE BUBBLE

Like many white institutions, Sewickley Academy has a history of exclusivity. At more than 175 years old, it's the oldest independent school in western Pennsylvania. It started as an all-boys school in 1838, closed during the Civil War, and reopened in 1865. The school became co-ed in 1925, admitting girls five years after white women won the right to vote. Growing up, it never occurred to me that I was attending a school that predated the Civil War, or that at my school's inception black men, women, and children were in chains. I know as America evolved, my school did too, but I'm curious to know what that evolution looked like. What had I, a pre-kindergartner in 1986, inherited? What was I walking into? I guess the answer is whiteness. I was walking into whiteness.

I was playing on the school playground one weekend—I must have been nine or ten—and ran into a boy who looked to be about seven or eight. He took one look at me and said, "What happened to your skin? Were you born that way?" The kids around me stopped and stared, as if they, too, had been wondering the same thing. I waited for someone to say something, to come to my rescue, but no one did. So I acted like it was a joke. Like something was wrong with him—not me. It was a hard act to pull off. Then a woman, who I assume was the boy's mother, standing on the opposite side of the fence outside of the playground, called the boy back to her. My discomfort lingered long after he left. Had this child really never seen a black person before? Did he really not know we existed? Was it possible he lived in a world seeing only faces that looked like his?

Then one day I was standing in the lunch line at school. I think I was in third grade. Two girls were standing in line behind me. One was telling the other about a trip she had recently been on and started showing off her tan line. She caught sight of me listening in on her conversation then placed her tanned hand next to mine. "I'm almost as dark as you are," she said. The other girl suppressed a smile and looked the other way. I wanted to disappear. I could almost feel myself shrinking. Was this racism? Rudeness? It felt more severe than that—more raw. But I didn't have a name for it. Not then, anyway. I just knew it made me feel awful. What's worse is that I didn't have the words to stop it. I didn't know how to respond or answer back. So I said nothing. I did nothing. To explain to white people why their words or actions are offensive is like speaking a whole new language, and I had yet to learn it. Instead I remained silent and still, soaking up what they spilled out.

Before we moved to Sewickley—or "the Bubble," as a friend in high school used to call it—my family and I lived with Grandma in Aliquippa, a town still suffering the aftershock of a declining steel industry. It wasn't until I was an adult that Mom told me how hard it had been for her and Dad to buy a house in Sewickley. On one occasion, they offered to pay exactly what was being asked, but then, after they did so, the house was taken off the market. Their real estate agent used very coded language to explain why the homeowners had changed their minds, but my parents knew why. They were black. The Bubble was white. So instead we moved into a three-bedroom apartment a few blocks away from school. I was five, I think. But we continued to visit Grandma and my aunt and uncle every weekend in Aliquippa where my sister and I would go to Sunday school at a black church, get our hair done at a black salon, take piano lessons from a black teacher, and play *UNO* with our black friends. I used to think

Aliquippa was a predominantly black town—it's not. Today, Aliquippa's black population is just under forty percent. But in Sewickley, it's less than nine.

In the Bubble we didn't talk about race in the present tense. Growing up, race was a thing of the past. In school we studied slavery, the Civil War, Reconstruction, and Jim Crow. We watched *Eyes on the Prize*, a documentary about the Civil Rights Movement. The story of African Americans didn't start with slavery and didn't end with civil rights, but according to our history books you'd think it had. That's another thing about living in the Bubble. It's full of blind spots.

In the fourteen years I attended the academy, the O.J. Simpson trial was the only racially charged event that came up in class. I was in eighth grade. I was sitting in Algebra when someone came in to announce the verdict. "Unbelievable," my teacher mumbled under her breath, shaking her head back and forth. Was it my imagination, or was she finding it hard to look at me? Or maybe it was the other way around. Maybe I was finding it hard to look at her. I remember how uncomfortable it was to sit in my seat, to occupy that space. I felt like I had done something wrong. Like I was the guilty one. Guilt by association. O.J. was black. And I was black. And this was a trial, or at least had become a trial, about race: black people versus white people. Black people had won, and white people weren't happy.

Later, in French class, before the bell rang, my friend Shannon tapped me on the shoulder, leaned forward in her seat, and said, "You know what's really unfair? It only takes nine people on a jury to reach a verdict, and nine of those jury members were black." I felt a stab of pain shoot straight through my chest. That was my fear: that I would be singled out because my race was the same as O.J.'s. Because Shannon's side had lost. But why did she think a predominantly black jury wouldn't convict a black defendant? And why would she feel the need to say it? To share it? To me? Her *one* black friend? White juries convict and acquit white defendants all the time without race being an issue. Why can't a black jury do the same? Shannon thought she was exposing bias when really she was revealing her own.

"Actually, it has to be unanimous," I said.

"No, it doesn't," she said.

"Yeah, it does," I said.

She turned to the boy next to her.

"She's right," he said. "It has to be unanimous."

Shannon shrugged her shoulders and looked the other way.

I knew it took all twelve jury members to reach a verdict. She, on the other hand, did not. She was wrong. I was right. That's the only reason I was able to answer back to her that day and not stay silent. I knew the facts. And those facts were undeniable. But today, it's never that simple. It's never that straightforward. Facts don't seem to matter as much as they used to. People pick and choose their facts in order to support the story they want to tell. Am I really a match for that?

A couple of years earlier Shannon invited me to her house for a slumber party where we watched the movie *Ladybugs*. There's a scene in the movie where Jackée Harry tells Rodney Dangerfield that black people are the best at sports, then named all of the sports in which black people dominated. In the movie, Rodney Dangerfield struggles to answer back to Jackée, so my friend Shannon did instead. She started naming sports in which she felt white people were the best. "Golf, tennis..." she said. This, of course, was before the days of Tiger, Venus, and Serena.

When Shannon was done defending the white race, no one said a thing, including me. I had been holding my breath, waiting for the moment to pass. I wonder if Shannon would have felt the need to say what she did if I hadn't been at the party. She was an athlete herself, after all, as was I. Was it some sort of competition? Did she feel threatened by what Jackée had said? Or threatened by me? I was the only black girl at the sleepover. Everyone else was white.

In both instances, the sleepover and the aftermath of the Simpson verdict, Shannon had been asserting her whiteness, and with that, her self-proclaimed superiority, and I had been the intended target. For black people, this is what life looks like from inside the Bubble. It's toxic. And traumatic. Toxicity is when words and actions go unexamined, power goes unquestioned, prejudice goes unnoticed, and privilege goes unchecked. And trauma is when toxicity goes untreated.

A few years ago, Mom sent me a cutout from the *Sewickley Herald*, the local paper. My school was screening a documentary in Rea Auditorium called *I'm Not Racist...Am I?* The event was free and open to the public. My guess, my hope, is that the school also showed the film during school hours, and every high school student saw it and then discussed it after. When I was in high school we did a screening of *Dead Man Walking* and then split into groups to debate the death penalty. I wonder, though, how comfortable black students are sharing their experiences, thoughts, and opinions on race in the presence of their white peers. I wonder if there are "All Lives Matter" students sitting in the seats next to them. I wonder if black students are confident enough to be vocal, or do they feel, as I did at that age, that it was all too much work.

In February we celebrated Black History Month. Ms. Banks was a black woman who taught sixth grade English but retired before I could be in her class. She coordinated the Black History Month program at my school. Actually, it wasn't a program—it was an event. *And it. Was. Lit.* I learned the Negro national anthem at Sewickley Academy's Black History Month celebration. *That's* how lit it was.

I was always asked to participate in the event. Students who were not asked to participate were encouraged to attend with their families. Some did. Most did not. There was always a play or performance piece to honor a renowned African American. A ceremony was held and some years a banquet, too. Hors d'oeuvres were served in the gallery outside of the auditorium, and everyone dressed up. My sister and I would run around in our Laura Ashley dresses with Renee, Humphrey, and the other black kids from the lower grades and eat all the pigs in a blanket.

The first year I participated we honored Gordon Parks, the photographer. We did a play about him with students of all ages. I was in first grade and had one line I shared with about a half a dozen other kids in case one of us forgot it: *Gordon's going to ask his papa for a nickel!* One year the artist Jimmy Denmark was featured. My parents bought a print of one of his paintings called "Easter Sunday." It hangs in their living room to this day. I remember one year sitting in Rea Auditorium and listening to two students from the senior school—one black, one white—sing "Ebony and Ivory." Then one year we all received a printout of the lyrics to "We Shall Overcome" and "Lift Every Voice and Sing," the Negro national anthem, and sang it together at the end of the ceremony. In fourth grade we did a play about a time machine that brought back famous black artists and activists. I played Alice Walker. I was in charge of greeting and intro-ducing the famed person as he or she stepped out of the time machine. I had twelve lines. Renee played Zora Neale Hurston. She had seven. When Renee stepped out of the time machine we embraced and gave each other a kiss on each cheek like the French do and everyone laughed.

The Black History Month event at my school reinforced what I already knew to be true, that black people are beau-tiful, that we deserve to be celebrated, and that I belong in any space a white person does. It acted as a healing agent to the slights I received as a child. It reminded me that I was in the right and they were in the wrong. It gave me a sense of community. It helped renew my sense of self. It allowed me to see myself, if only a fraction of myself, and like what I saw. Perhaps most of all, it taught me that it was okay to assert my blackness in white spaces. That I can show pride in who I am and where I come from. That I don't need to lessen myself to make others feel more comfortable. That I don't need to hide. Lessons I'm still grappling with today.

It also taught me that a white institution can create a space, a sense of community for black people, celebrate Black History Month, even hold a meet and greet at the start of the school year for new students of color to attend, and *still* be unconsciously biased. This is the Bubble, after all. It's possible to be progressive and problematic at the same time. I'm not sure everyone knew that. I'm not sure everyone knew that separating the black children from one another and putting them in different classrooms may have created a sense of diversity for the white kids, but it only isolated the black kids. I'm not sure everyone knew that a little black girl could show up for school every day and feel that isolation in reading circle, on the playground, and in the lunch line. I don't know if everyone sitting in Rea Auditorium, listening to "Ebony and Ivory" understood that. I'm not sure they wanted to. And I'm not sure everyone singing "We Shall Overcome" knew exactly what was needed for overcoming: white people to take a hard look at themselves.

After Ms. Banks retired from teaching, Black History Month was not the celebration it had been. Sixth grade was the last year I participated in it. I have no memory of it at all in middle school or high school. Middle school was a rough time for me. I had friends, but I felt out of place. It wasn't until I started getting heavily involved in theater that I really began to step into myself, to find my voice, but even then I had to hide behind a character. It's where I felt safest. Still, the Black History Month celebration had left its mark on me. In seventh grade I was inspired to write a poem called "200 Years Into Slavery" after visiting an African American art and history museum with my family. I brought the poem into school to show my English teacher, as well as a quilt I had made to go along with it, patterns of people floating on clouds drifting off into an endless sky. She asked that I read the poem out loud to the rest of the class, which was no easy feat, particularly at that age, when you practically breathe self-consciousness, and you have a history of being humiliated because of the color of your skin. Still, I stood up and did it anyway. I had a need to assert my blackness, if only a little at a time.

200 YEARS INTO SLAVERY
Melva Graham
Seventh Grade

It began in Africa our Motherland
Our culture, our language, our dancing in the sand
Our celebrations, our customs, our own special ways
Then the Americans[1] came along and threw it all away
They put us in chains, threw us deep down in a ship
Where some of us died or got very sick
We reached a new land that we did not know
Then they sold us as property and stuck us in small cabins they called our home
They gave us new names, and when we would not accept them they whipped us with whips and canes

[1] My use of the word "Americans" was really my way of being politically correct. I wanted to say white people, but I also didn't want to shame or alienate anyone in my class, including my teacher. I'm so considerate when it comes to white people. Even at such a young age I could recognize in myself a need to assert my blackness but in a manner that would not be alarming or offensive to the white people around me.

They stuck us in fields and put us to work
Then they left us to lie in the dirt
There were the people who could fly but others would just run
But truly our 200 years of slavery has now begun
From then on it was torture, pain, and sorrow
Yet we still had hope for a better tomorrow
Days, months, years went by
There was a Civil War and we had hope that slavery would die
More days, months, years passed
The Civil War ended we were free at last
Our 200 years of slavery has now passed

What strikes me most about writing that poem is that no one asked me to do it. It wasn't a homework assignment or an attempt to earn extra credit. We weren't studying the Civil War in history or poetry in English. My church wasn't having a special evening service about African American heritage, and it wasn't Black History Month. I simply did it just to do it. It's moments like those I hold on to. Moments I can look back on and smile. Moments that reveal who I am, or at least, who I strive to be. I love this part of me. The part that so badly wants to be the whole of who I am. I didn't realize it at the time, but writing that poem, bringing it into class, showing my teacher, and reading it in front of my peers was a small act of courage. As if to say, "I will be seen. I will be heard." I remember my thirteen-year-old self as someone who just wanted to fit in—if only I could fit in—and yet, there I was doing something that would make me stand out.

In eighth grade, we had to memorize eight lines of Martin Luther King's "I Have a Dream" speech. Each of us had to stand behind a podium and recite it in front of our history class. For every line you learned thereafter you would receive an extra credit point. I memorized the whole thing. Every. Single. Word. Not that my grade needed it. I did it so that if I ever experienced stage fright before a play or performance

I could say to myself, "Melva, if you can recite the entire 'I Have a Dream' speech then you can do this." And so I did. The speech was two pages long, front and back, and ran just over fifteen minutes. As I was saying it, I remember how hard it was to make eye contact with my classmates. I knew I was doing something special but I couldn't quite own up to it. I couldn't quite stand in my full power. I still remember the reaction of my classmates as they realized I was going to recite the entire thing. Their look of shock and awe as they scanned the pages with their finger, following along, line by line, on their copy of the text. And then the resounding applause when I finished, the impressed faces, the standing ovation by my teachers. It still makes me smile when I think about it. Teachers congratulated me as if I had written the speech myself. They weren't my words, only a recitation of someone more powerful—someone who had a voice.

A few years earlier, when I was around ten or so, Humphrey's mom opened up a store in Sewickley called "The A Connection." The store sold African-inspired merchandise. My family went to the grand opening. I remember buying a hat and a jewelry dish with my own money. I'm pretty sure if you go through some of the drawers in my parents' house you'll find a set of old playing cards with an African-inspired print on the back and the face of a black King, Queen, Jack, and Joker on the front. The store didn't last long, but when I think about it today, I can't help but appreciate the need so many of us had to assert our blackness in a predominantly white space. That, I think, is key. As a black child, as a black adult, if you can do that you can do anything. Me? I'm still working on it. The need to assert myself—my blackness—is there, but for me to do it is a challenge. I think what it comes down to is permission. I have a need to ask for permission. Maybe that's what made reciting the entire MLK speech so uncomfortable (and so remarkable). No one asked me to do the whole thing, but I did it anyway.

Today, I'm told I live in the Liberal Bubble, this open-door oasis with juice bars, yoga mats, kale, and soul cycle, where like-minded, forward-thinking, politically correct people can close their eyes and breathe for up to twenty minutes at a time and not be bothered by bigots. But you can live in the Bubble and still be biased. You can be on the right side of history and still be biased. I have several friends who have said something I have taken offense to, or rubbed me the wrong way, or made me sick to my stomach, but who remain progressive in their political views and vote the same way I do. If I live in a bubble it's a pretty shitty bubble. There are a lot of white tears in the Bubble too. White people who complain that they're being discriminated against. White people who think the system is rigged against them. When you live in the Bubble, white tears fall from the sky. In fact, I need to wear a life vest so as not to drown, because if I call it out, if I yell, "Help! I'm drowning!" the following happens: defensiveness, denial, defeat. The people crying refuse to believe I'm drowning in their tears, or they admit I *am* drowning but believe they had nothing to do with it, or they accept that I'm drowning and that they *are* a part of the problem, which in turn makes them cry harder. Then I end up consoling them *while I drown*. I used to want to break free from the Bubble— today I just want to build my own—but as far as I know, the only bubble built for black people is Wakanda, and that, I hear, is really hard to get to.

FOR THE CULTURE

In the 80s and 90s, black female artists gave me life. *Life*. It was monumental seeing Diana Ross as Dorothy in *The Wiz*, Keshia Knight Pulliam as the titular role in *Polly*, and Brandy, star in the remake of *Cinderella*. I remember seeing Vanessa Lee Chester in *A Little Princess*, and how meaningful it was that a little black girl was included in a story about little white girls. I loved those stories, and seeing myself reflected in their image, knowing that they were made and meant for me, gave me a real sense of power and purpose.

I used to think I'd be discovered next, spotted on the streets of Sewickley. I used to think Spielberg or Spike Lee would pass through my small suburban town, see me buying candy at the Sweet Shoppe, and think, *That's her, that's the one, the one we've been looking for*. Then they'd fly me off to New York or Los Angeles to shoot my first movie. I used to imagine my name popping up on the big screen. Nightly entertainment shows would refer to me as "Newcomer Melva Graham, in her breakout role…." I used to think all this would happen by the time I started high school, that I'd be eating lunch with Tia and Tamera Mowry (*I say your name*), Keshia Knight Pulliam (*I say your name*), and Tatyana Ali (*I say your name*). I used to think that they were my people. And that wherever they were was where I belonged.

To me, Hollywood—black Hollywood—felt closer than it was. That's what TV, music, and movies do. They make your dreams feel alive, come alive. I don't remember when I started to dream but when I did, I dreamed of more. Having more. Being more. Something more. I wanted to sing like Whitney Houston, dance like Janet Jackson, and act like Whoopi Goldberg. I thought those women spoke to me—and only me. I was wrong, of course. They spoke to every little black girl, and every little black boy, who looked at those women and saw themselves. Hollywood—black Hollywood—was this place of possibility. Where we could have black Dorothys, and black Pollys, and black Cinderellas. It wasn't a lot—it never is—but it was something, and to a little black girl going to a white school, living in a white town, it was everything.

After seeing movies like *Polly* and *The Wiz*, I began to think that was who we were. That was what we did. We took white stories, and we made them our own. I began to do the same. I used to reimagine my favorite stories with all black characters. In truth, I still have this tendency as an adult and am slightly embarrassed by it. It's a strange source of comfort. I do it unknowingly. I'll suddenly find myself daydreaming the happenings in a beloved story, see nothing but faces that look like mine, and then recoil at the meaning behind the message: a longing for inclusiveness, a need to see my face in the stories I relate to.

When I was young, one of my favorite characters was Pippi Longstocking. My sister and I turned her into a black girl named Poppi Shortsocks. Poppi's adventures became my own. I let her live inside my head. My sister and I rewrote the lyrics to the theme song to make her story even more real to us; then we ran throughout our apartment singing, over and over again, our voices ringing out....

Poppi Shortsocks is coming into your world
A curly-haired brown-skinned girl you oughta know
She's going to change your world....

In fourth grade we did a small in-class performance of *Harriet the Spy* after reading the book by Louise Fitzhugh. Each student had to write down on a sheet of paper which two parts they would most like to play. I, like the rest of the girls in my class, wrote down Harriet as my first choice, and Golly, her nanny, as my second. My teacher chose *me* as Harriet. *I couldn't believe it.* A girl from another class asked who was playing Harriet and I remember the look of shock on her face when I told her it was me. In truth, I was as shocked as she was. Earlier that year I had been cast as a grasshopper and was convinced it was because I was the tallest and had the longest legs. I had thought that the part of Harriet would go to the girl who *looked* most like Harriet. In other words, not me. I was only nine or ten, and yet, I had already begun to believe this lie about myself. That the color of my skin was in some way limiting. That it prevented me from being who I wanted to be. At least in that instance, it turned out to be untrue. That day, in fourth grade, Harriet the Spy was black. And why shouldn't she be?

Then, in high school, I saw Vanessa Lee Chester in *The Lost World: Jurassic Park*, playing the daughter of Jeff Goldblum. I had never seen anything like that before. Sure, I'd seen black women play traditionally white roles—Diana Ross, Keshia Knight Pulliam, Brandy—but not like that. Not in a family setting. Not when the rest of the world remained white. It was like me being cast as Harriet. Only it wasn't in a classroom. It was in a movie. I couldn't quite wrap my brain around it. Neither could my friend. When the movie was over she had a bewildered look on her face, "Why would they do that?" she asked. She wanted to know why they would cast a black girl to play the daughter of a white man. She thought I might know the answer, but I didn't. I just knew I was happy they did. This was a Steven Spielberg major motion picture. If there was space for her, then there was space for me.

Or so I thought.

Or so I believed.

But there's always someone to remind you.

To tell you. Otherwise.

My friend Adam. He has two favorite stories he likes to tell about me to large groups of people. The first is how freshman year in college I could get wasted drinking half a bottle of Zima. The second is that after encouraging my acting studio to read the Harry Potter books and then see the first movie opening weekend, I suggested we show up to the theater dressed as characters from the book. (Naturally, naturally.) I had insisted on being Harry and asked Adam to dye his hair red to go as Ron. "Uh, Melva," he'd say, to a crowd of people breathing in his every word, "Do you not realize you're a black woman? And yet you want to go as Harry? But you want me to dye my hair red to go as Ron?"

I hate that story.

And look, I get it. Adam, a white boy with dark brown hair, looks more like Harry than I do. There. I said it. But I was going to wear glasses and draw a lightning-bolt-shaped scar on my forehead and wear a Hogwarts scarf around my neck. People would know that I was Harry. Right? And if they didn't know, believe me, I would tell them. How would they know Adam was Ron if he didn't dye his hair red, I reasoned. I don't know…maybe I was wrong. Maybe dyeing his hair red was too much to ask. Maybe it would have made more sense for Adam to go as Harry and for me to go as Angelina Johnson, the only black-identified female character in the series. But why do I have to be reduced to the color of my skin when I'm playing pretend. Don't I get enough of that in life? Why does it have to happen in my imagination too?

When it was announced that Noma Dumezweni, a black English actress, would be playing the role of Hermione Granger in London's West End production of *Harry Potter and the Cursed Child* there was a lot of backlash—a lot of racist backlash. But there was also a lot of praise and support, most notably from the author J.K. Rowling herself, and

Emma Watson, the actress who originated the role on screen. I thought of my friend Adam and felt somewhat vindicated. I was delighted, but also—hard as it is to admit—disconcerted. Delighted because a black woman was playing Hermione Granger. Disconcerted because, well, a black woman was playing Hermione Granger. Stay with me on this.

I had always imagined the Harry Potter trio as white. And now I was being asked to see Hermione differently. To see her as black. It's something we are rarely asked to do. To see a traditionally white character as a character of color, and then to integrate that character into a story, a world, dominated by white characters. I'd spent fifteen years reading the Harry Potter books. Fifteen years of imagining Harry, Ron, and Hermione inside my head. Fifteen years in the corridors, the classrooms, the common rooms of Hogwarts. Now, fifteen years later, as an adult, I am told that one of the Harry Potter trio is black. I mean, COME ON. It would have been nice if this had happened at the start of the story when I was a teenager. It would have been nice to know that one of the most famous female characters in children's literature could be brilliant, bold, *and* BLACK. After all, if I can't see Noma Dumezweni as Hermione, then I can't see myself as Hermione either.

A few years out of college I was asked to do an imagination exercise in an acting class. The teacher dimmed the lights and told us to close our eyes. She then walked us through a make-believe scenario in which we were to imagine having and caring for a small child of our own. The child that popped into my head was white. I tried to reimagine her as black but was finding it hard to do so. When the exercise was over the teacher asked us to talk about our experience. I stayed silent. I was too embarrassed that I was unable to imagine having a child that looked like me. A young Asian woman sitting a few seats away from me raised her hand and spoke, "I had a hard time with this exercise. I kept imagining a little white girl."

I wasn't the only one.

Thank God, I wasn't the only one.

Years later, when I taught acting to kids in Los Angeles, I was coaching a young boy who was up for a lead role in a feature film based on a popular middle grade novel. In the middle of the coaching session, the boy said to me, "I was surprised they called me in for this role. When I read the book, I kept picturing a white boy with blond hair. Not some Filipino boy."

I said to him what I would have wanted someone to say to me. "Well, it looks like someone else read the book and pictured you."

If your imagination, like mine, like the imagination of the little boy I was coaching, like the imagination of the young woman in my acting class, has been whitewashed, if there have been rules and restrictions on who you can and cannot be in the world of make-believe, your imagination becomes limited, and so you, in turn, become limited. What we read, what we watch, inspires our imagination, informs our imagination and how we see others and ourselves. The problem is, the dominant culture controls and creates the stories we consume, which means my imagination is subject to theirs, and that's a dangerous thing. Yes, a part of me, the part that champions black excellence was—and will always be—delighted when a black person is cast in a traditionally white role, but another part of me, the part that has been told *you're breaking the rules, this isn't how we do things,* is disconcerted. That's why I was stunned when I was cast as Harriet the Spy, and when I saw Vanessa Lee Chester playing the daughter of Jeff Goldblum, and when I read that Noma Dumezweni had been cast as Hermione Granger. I ended up having the same thought about Noma Dumezweni that my friend Adam had about me. Why? Because I didn't think such a thing was possible. I responded in the way the dominant culture has trained me to. And I can't stand it. I shouldn't be disconcerted. And I shouldn't beat myself up over it either. But I am. And I do.

A few years after black Hermione broke the Internet, I was binge-watching the second season of *Stranger Things*. In episode two the four boys dress up as Ghostbusters for Halloween, and both Mike, the leader of the group, and Lucas, the only black boy in the group, show up with a name tag that says Venkman. Mike thought Lucas was going as Winston, the black Ghostbuster. Lucas says he never agreed to that. They go back and forth, arguing over who should be who. Lucas tells Mike to go as Winston. Mike says he can't be Winston because he's... But he's unable to finish his sentence. Lucas finishes it for him... Because you're not black? Then Mike gets defensive. He says he didn't say that. Lucas says no, but you thought it. And in my opinion, if he's thinking I can't be Winston because I'm not black then he's also thinking you can't be Venkman because you're not white...I loved this moment. This rare insight into 1980s black suburban life. Of course Lucas wouldn't want to go as Winston, as he says in the scene, "He joined the team super late. He's not funny, and he's not even a scientist." Lucas would want to go as Venkman, the cool, confident leader of the pack. But no, as a black kid his white friend saw him as Winston, the black dude.

For a person of color, inclusiveness has always come with a set of conditions. You want to play Harry Potter? You can't be Harry. You have to be the black girl. You want to play Ghostbusters? You can't be Venkman. You have to be the black guy. The thing is there's only ever one. One black girl. One black guy. In a white space. Imaginary or not. One spot. One opportunity for an entire generation of black boys and black girls who dream the same dream. What does that do to an entire community when there is only one seat at the table? Do we work with one another or against one another? Are we collaborators or competitors?

Look. I know that whether I get to play Harry Potter or Harriet the Spy in a game of make-believe is not a priority. Al Sharpton won't bring it up. He refuses to take my calls. I get it. I know that we as a community have bigger concerns, bigger issues, but as a black child, this was my concern, this was my issue. Can I be whoever I want to be? Some said yes, others said no. Where did that leave me? Where does that leave any black child who—as I did—uses make-believe and imaginary play to dream up a world in which they not only belong but are the heroes of their own story?

I want—I need—to see more black women in traditionally white roles until I'm just delighted and no longer disconcerted, until it becomes the norm and there is nothing to be disconcerted about. We've had black Dorothy, black Polly, black Cinderella, black Annie, black Hermione. I want black Matilda and black Mary Poppins. I want black Belle and black Ariel. I want black Wendy Moira Angela Darling. I want black Eloise at the Plaza. I want the girl in *Charlotte's Web* to be black. I want a black remake of *Honey, I Shrunk the Kids*. Just because. I want Meg, Jo, Beth, and Amy to all be black. I want a black Anne of Green Gables. I want Elizabeth and Jane Bennet to be black. I don't care about the historical accuracy of it all. I want them to be black. I want it. All black. All black everything.

For the culture.

For the people.

For myself.

A SEAT AT THE LUNCH TABLE

If you were to ask me what I was like as a child, I would say I was the same person then that I am now. Quiet, reserved, sometimes shy. But in truth, I don't know if that's who I was at all. I think that's who I needed to be in order to survive the space I was in. It makes me wonder. Who might I have been had I not needed to adjust to my surroundings? Had I let my surroundings adjust to me?

A few summers ago I was home visiting Mom and Dad in Sewickley and found a box of old report cards in the garage. I sat on the cement and went through them one by one. And as I did, something broke inside me. That something was the belief I've had, the belief I've held, for so long, for so many years, that I wasn't enough, that I didn't belong. It is—it was—a core belief, and I could feel it, after so many years, crack open, in an instant, and start to crumble, as I wept from the wound, and read the words written on the page.

In second grade my teacher, Miss Perry, wrote, "Melva is an excellent citizen. She is very cooperative and polite. Classroom participation is excellent. Work habits are marvelous. Melva is a friendly girl and is always willing to help other students. She is more popular than she realizes." As an adult, it makes me sad. To know I underestimated myself even as a child. To know my teacher saw something in me that I couldn't see myself. I know everyone wants to fit in, but when you're an "other" you want it more. Or maybe, it just means more. It means you belong. Because for so long you never thought you did. I never thought I did.

I remember sitting across from Miss Perry during our student-teacher conference. What she said took me by surprise.

"Melva, I know you have a very good friend in the room across the hall." She was talking about Renee. "But," she went on to say, "there are a lot of students in our classroom who would really like to be your friend, too." *There are? Like who?* "In all my years of teaching," she continued, "I've never seen anyone more popular on Halloween." Now that made me smile. That year I had walked into school dressed as Janet Jackson for Halloween. I carried a red microphone, wore Mom's black leather jacket, and clipped on a pair of star-shaped diamond studded earrings. I spent recess signing autographs, striking a pose, saying, "Give me a beat!" and then doing what I thought was the choreography to "Rhythm Nation," which in my mind was the running man on repeat. At the Halloween assembly, students walked up on stage with their class and said who they were in front of the entire Lower School. When I leaned into the microphone and said Janet Jackson, everyone cheered.

The following year, Renee went as Paula Abdul, and I remember being annoyed thinking she had kind of copied me from the year before. As each year passed, my friendship with her became more and more strained. We'd give each other the silent treatment, and then a few days later we'd start talking again. In fourth grade she and another girl made up a rhyme about me. *Melva is a disgrace to the human race.* Somehow, we went back to being friends after that.

I don't know why I stuck with Renee for as long as I did. It's possible that with Renee I thought the color of my skin would never be an issue as it had been with some of my white classmates. But that turned out to be untrue. It was an issue or at least became one. Our shared color turned us into competitors.

In sixth grade, Renee and I made a pact one Monday morning to be one of the popular girls by the end of the day Friday. The popular girls had been popular since third grade.

For some reason, Renee and I thought that what they had achieved in three years we could pull off in five days. I had no such luck, but Renee was making notable strides as the week progressed. I remember how easy it was for her to draw attention to herself. Something I could never do. By the end of the week Renee was sitting with the popular girls at the lunch table. I, on the other hand, was not. I thought Renee might help me get in with the group, but when I mentioned it, her face fell. "My mom said they're only going to let in one of us." I hadn't thought of that, but I knew immediately what she meant. I had thought that there was room for both of us. That there were enough seats at the table. But Renee's mother knew better. She had passed on a hard and hurtful truth to her daughter, and her daughter passed it on to me. *Two black women can't share the same space.*

Was that why it was so hard for me to be happy for her? Because I knew her success meant I had failed? That if she became popular then I could not? If she wins then I lose? Is this what happens when you move through white spaces? You have to compete with those around you? With other black people? Is there really only one seat at the table? I didn't argue. I didn't protest. I knew deep down she was right, and I was wrong. Four white girls were only going to befriend one black girl. Not two. That's the way it was on TV and in movies. That's the way it was in life. There was only ever one. And that one was going to be Renee.

The new narrative is that there's room for all of us. When one person wins we all win. That's the message but I don't know if that's the mentality. The mentality is still that there is only one spot, one seat at the table, to be filled by someone *like* you but not necessarily you. It's hard not to think it's intentional. To pit people of color against one another. To turn us into tokens.

I hate the word token.

I hate being one even more.

In high school I was at the movies with a group of friends and saw a preview for *Not Another Teen Movie*, a parody on all the teen movies that had recently been released. In the trailer, a black character is introduced as the Token Black Guy. My friends found it funny. I did not. I took it personally. Like *I* was the one being laughed at. I saw myself in him. How could I not? I was the only black girl in a group of white girls going to a white school in a white town. What did that make me? Was I a token too? According to society, I am. That's what white people have made me out to be. Melva Graham. The token. The only black person in the room. In fact, one of the few times I'm not the only black person in the room is when I'm auditioning. I walk into these rooms all the time, rooms filled with women who look like me, each one holding a headshot and resume, each one desperate to be seen, desperate to be heard.

I've tried hard not to hold on to the message Renee left, that there can be only one, but I'm not sure how well I'm do-ing. It continues to come up, but I'm starting to let it go. It's a slow process. I know the fault is not my own. And I know it's not hers or her mother's either. I must remember that and add a little compassion to the criticism. I'm taking the blame off myself, off of us, and placing it where it belongs—in the hands of white people. (Yes, white people.) Those who created the system I'm working—we, the black community, are working—to dismantle.

In the end, Renee's friendship with the popular girls lasted only long enough for the two of us to drift apart for good. I never sat at the lunch table with them, but it turned out I didn't need to. Miss Perry had been right. I found another group of girls who remained my friends until graduation.

Two of whom I'm still friends with today. As for Renee, she left Sewickley Academy at the end of seventh grade. I haven't spoken to her in years but I hope wherever she is, whatever she's doing, she's being seen, she's being heard, and she has a seat at whichever table she'd like to sit.

AN (AFRICAN) AMERICAN TALE

I often hear white actors complain about how ethnicity is "really in" right now. It's true that the entertainment industry has made meaningful attempts to increase ethnic visibility—*however*, increasing characters of color does not diminish characters *without* color. This is what white actors don't seem to understand. White characters aren't going anywhere. It's not a trend. It's mainstream. White actors need never worry—*never*. The casting process is inherently discriminatory and works in their favor. Casting is prejudiced. The entire system is built on bias. Mr. Veshio taught me that.

He was the song and dance teacher. A former Broadway dancer with perfect posture and gray slicked-back hair. For thirty years he directed the school musicals. He might have been one of my most influential teachers. He instilled in me a deep love and appreciation for the arts. He used to make us watch old productions of his on VHS, then comment on his past students' performance so we'd know what to do and what not to do. When he forgot our names he'd call us Cuckoo or Kiki. He introduced me to Broadway's most memorable melodies and often singled me out in class for being the only one to remember the choreography from the week before. He was one of my favorites but I was never one of his.

In sixth grade we did the play *An American Tail*, based on the 1986 animated film. I had one line. I was disappointed but not altogether surprised when I read the names of my classmates listed under the roles I had auditioned for. I had tried out for two roles and hadn't been called back for either. I had even received private coaching for the scenes and songs I had to prepare. Mrs. Matthews, a black woman with dreads in her hair, was the founder and director of Messengers of the Future, a kid performance troupe my sister and I belonged to outside of school. We traveled to community centers and schools reading poetry, singing, dancing, and performing pieces that were reflective of our African American history and heritage. She took the time one day to help me prepare for my audition. Her son, Darius, also a member of the troupe, was in my grade and was auditioning for the lead role of Fievel.

Darius was the most racially aware kid I knew. He came up to me once in the cafeteria, picked up the napkin holder, and said in a strong preacher-like voice something like, "Don't forget it is the *black* napkin holder that is needed to hold the *white* napkins up! The *white* napkins would be nowhere without the *black* napkin holder!" My friends stared at him blankly while I struggled to keep a smile off my face.

Darius was also a strong singer. His voice was deep and resonant. The role of Fievel came down to him and Tanner, a tiny white boy with blond hair. Tanner knew all the lyrics to Tag Team's "Whoomp! (There It Is)," and often led the sixth grade class in a rousing rendition on the school bus to and from field trips until the teachers banned the song for its "inappropriateness."

In order to determine who would win the role of Fievel both Darius and Tanner had to sing Fievel's solo, "Somewhere Out There." In the end, Mr. Veshio gave the role of Fievel to Tanner, and he cast Darius as...

...*the cockroach.*

There was only one cockroach.

And Darius was it.

His parents pulled him from the play.

Then, Mr. Veshio cast an Indian girl to take Darius's place.

Why was this man so determined to cast a kid of color in the role of the cockroach? It's amazing to me that in a play about rodents where most of the cast members are playing mice, a few are playing cats, and a couple are playing birds, the one lesser creature is assigned to a black kid, and then, when he turns it down, is given to a brown kid.

Darius sat in the back of the auditorium doing homework or reading a book while the rest of the sixth graders went over blocking, learned choreography, and reviewed musical numbers for the show. It felt slightly uncomfortable, wrong even, that he should have to sit out by himself. I wonder what might have happened if all the black kids had decided to boycott the play and sit out in solidarity, but I know such a thing would never have happened. Humphrey, for one, had a small solo he would have been unlikely to give up, and, even with my one measly line, it would have been torture for me to sit out and watch the rest of my class on stage.

Tech week, the long week of rehearsals before opening night, was always the hardest part for me to endure as a young aspiring actress. It was the week the leads got the most attention, testing out their microphones on stage beneath the spotlight while the ensemble sat in the auditorium, doing their homework or drifting off to sleep. I remember this feeling most of all—wanting to wear a microphone and needing to test it out for the techies in the sound booth and the audience below. I wanted a part that warranted a microphone. I wanted to be someone who had something to say, someone who needed to be heard, someone who had a voice.

In the final days before opening night I sat on stage with the rest of the sixth graders (minus one), our throats sore from singing, our energy drained from dancing. Mr. Veshio was standing in the aisle of the auditorium, speaking into a handheld microphone to the teachers and moms who had volunteered to help. They were having a conversation about costumes and make-up, how to get us all to look like mice. We were to wear mouse noses, mouse ears, and mouse tails. He said he wanted our faces to be covered in white powder, and our eyebrows and whiskers outlined and exaggerated with black eyeliner. The teachers and moms nodded their heads in agreement. Then Mr. Veshio said, "Now, what do we do about the colored kids?" And my body turned to stone.

The colored kids?
He's talking about me.
He's talking about the black kids.
And the color of our skin.
Like there's something wrong with it.
Like there's something wrong with us.

I was only twelve, but I had a deep understanding of the word "colored," and the way it was used to describe black people. There was a time the word was seen on doors with signs that read, No Coloreds Allowed. It was used to keep black people out of places we were told we didn't belong. It was used to separate the races. Perhaps that's why Mr. Veshio invoked it. He was separating us after all. Distinguishing us from our peers—our white peers—in order to pinpoint a problem that needed to be solved.

The moms and teachers seemed to stiffen a bit. Mr. Veshio, perhaps picking up on this, turned his microphone off, before continuing his train of thought, and then, as always, life carried on as usual.

And so the *children of color* received different makeup than the white kids. I struggle to understand what the thinking had been. Perhaps if we, too, were given white powder to cover our faces, we would be appearing in white face or something like it, and that would be inappropriate? Or perhaps I'm giving Mr. Veshio too much credit. He might have just thought white powder wouldn't look good on us. Two years prior, my sister had been in the running for the role of the Blue Fairy in her sixth-grade production of *Pinocchio* but didn't get the part. When asked why, Mr. Veshio said something about how the Blue Fairy had to wear a blonde wig. So this was familiar ground.

On opening night I graced the stage with the rest of my sixth grade class (minus one), in a play rooted in the American Dream and the struggle behind it (both onstage and off). I listened for my cue and then turned to the audience. Speaking loud and clear, I uttered the one and only line assigned to me and perhaps the most poignant line in the entire play, "But what if we don't like it in America?" Yes, little mouse, what *if* we don't like it in America? What do we do? Do we pack up and leave? Do we stay and tough it out? Or do we turn it into a place we *do* like? In the play, my question goes unanswered, but, as I think about Darius and his willingness to sit out and be seen as a bad sport rather than be subjected to someone else's version of himself, I realize he answered my question for me after all.

Mr. Veshio died in 2008 at the age of seventy-eight. I happened to be home visiting my family at the time. I showed up to his memorial service with two childhood friends to honor him, ready to relive the days of musical theater arts camp and after-school dance classes. It seemed significant that I should find myself back there. I had recently moved to Los Angeles to pursue a passion I had discovered in that very room. But, sitting in Rea Auditorium, listening to his two teenage granddaughters sing "For Good" from *Wicked*, all I could think about was the time he said the Blue Fairy had to wear a blonde wig, and the time he cast a black boy and then an Indian girl to play the cockroach in our school musical, and the time he referred to me and the other black kids in my grade as "colored." And I'm like, what am I doing here? Why am I showing up for someone who never showed up for me?

Who can say if I've been changed for the better?

But because I knew you I have been changed for good.[2]

---

[2] Schwartz, Stephen. "For Good," *Wicked*. Decca Broadway, 2003.

43

NOTES FROM THE DIRECTOR

PART ONE: HIGH SCHOOL

In eleventh grade I did a play called *An American Daughter* by Wendy Wasserstein and was given the part of Judith, one of the leads. It was a race-specific role, requiring the actor who played the part to be black, putting the rest of my classmates out of the running. One day, during rehearsal, my high school acting teacher and director of the school play, Mr. Burke, was giving notes. I had just finished doing my monologue and was awaiting his feedback. He sat on the opposite end of the room, a look of exasperation on his face.

"I need you to make her more black," he said to me.

I hesitated a moment, unsure of what to say next. The class watched closely, took in every word, and received the same message I did. *I'm not black enough. Melva's not black enough.*

I've never heard a director tell a white actor they need to make a character more white or that they themselves were not acting white enough. Whiteness is expansive. I, on the other hand, seem to exist outside the parameters of blackness, or who my race allows me to be. I'm told I'm out of bounds and need to step back in line. White people have such a narrow, limited view of black people that, having grown up in predominantly white surroundings, I felt strangled by it.

Who else in my life looked at me the way Burke did?

I nodded my head curtly and said, "Okay," as if I knew exactly what he wanted me to do and was prepared to do it. I thought if I conveyed understanding he might drop the subject and turn his attention to someone else. And he did. But I didn't take his stupid note. I didn't change my performance. I didn't diminish myself so that his idea of blackness could be sustained. I did, however, harbor a hurt so deep I began to lose myself in it.

When you're a black girl and you're sixteen and you're too tall and you're too skinny and you wear braces and you have to stand in front of your classmates—your white classmates—while they listen to your teacher—your white teacher—tell you you're not black enough, not enough of who you already are, it isn't just humiliating, it's demoralizing. The only time I felt comfortable—confident—in my own skin at that age was when I was on stage, because I knew I had something to offer. Suddenly that security slipped away, and my self-consciousness slid into shame.

It wasn't the first time Burke had singled me out, calling my blackness into question. The year before, I had arrived to class one day and had taken a seat in the circle of chairs in the middle of the room.

"Melva," Burke said, his eyes rolling over me. "Where are your 3AC colors?"

3AC was the African American Awareness Club, and that day each of its members were to wear colors indicative of their African heritage. Simone, a black girl in my class, was dressed head to toe in hers.

Apparently Burke thought 3AC was only for black students, and that only we needed to be aware of African American history and heritage, because he didn't ask any of the white kids where their 3AC colors were.

"I'm not in 3AC," I said, feeling more than a little uncomfortable for being called out and having all eyes placed on me and my wardrobe selection.

Something told me Burke already knew I wasn't in 3AC but used this as an opportunity to draw attention to the matter anyway.

"Oh," he said, his voice dripping with judgment.

Perhaps, because I had attended a predominantly white

school since pre-kindergarten, he thought it had caused me to assimilate, and therefore forget where I came from, forget who I was. Perhaps he thought I was disconnected from the black community. Perhaps he thought I wasn't in the African American Awareness Club, because I was unaware that I was African American, and it was his job to remind me.

And remind me he did.

Later that year he pulled me aside in the hallway as I was making my way to class, accompanied by a friend and fellow acting bud. "Have you picked out a new monologue yet?" Burke asked. I shook my head. "I think you should do an African American piece," he said.

I suddenly became very aware of myself and my surroundings, standing face-to-face with a middle-aged white man and beside my white friend, who apparently didn't need any further advice on her choice of monologue but was allowed to choose her own.

"How about August Wilson?" I suggested.

Burke grimaced. "August Wilson is kinda white."

What?! August Wilson? Who chronicles black American life throughout the twentieth century? *Is kinda white?!*

I was dumbfounded. Burke didn't offer up any suggestions as to what an African American piece or who an African American playwright *really* was. No alternatives were mentioned. It was more like, I'll know it when I see it, and August Wilson wasn't it.

It seemed neither Wilson nor I was up to Burke's standards as to what it meant to be black. At least I was in good company.

In twelfth grade we did Shakespeare's *A Midsummer Night's Dream*. I was not cast as Helena (as I had hoped) or Titania (as I would have liked). Instead, I was cast as Nick Bottom, otherwise known as the ass, a mechanic who falls in love with

Titania, queen of the fairies, and whose head is magically transformed into a donkey.

I couldn't do it. I just. Couldn't. Do it.

The girl who had been cast as Titania was pretty and popular, much nicer than the other popular girls at my school, but still, I couldn't bring myself to take on the role of one of her suitors and gallop behind her, behaving like a donkey. In the play, Titania and Bottom's love story is intentional mockery, comic relief; somehow in that instance I couldn't allow myself to be the butt of the joke. To fawn over the pretty, popular white girl while I played Bottom, the undesirable, unpopular black girl. It felt demeaning. I couldn't stand on stage next to her while she acted like a queen and I an ass.

I dropped out of the play, like Darius had done when he was cast as the cockroach. But I didn't have the guts to say why. I was afraid I'd be misunderstood. Instead I said I wanted to concentrate on my college applications and prepare for my auditions. I had to take a stand. It felt uncomfortable to do so, but the alternative would have been far worse. Burke was not pleased. But, then again, neither was I.

I realize now it was my own insecurity with race and identity that prevented me from playing the part. After all, Bottom is a great role, and had I played it, I would have nailed it. But I had been humiliated and hurt so many times for being nothing more than myself. Why would that time be any different? I thought that accepting the role meant I was setting myself up for ridicule. How would people respond if I took on the role of a donkey? How would they look at me? I know I was overly concerned with people's perception of me, but how could I not be when their perception of me seemed to hold more power than my perception of myself?

I felt like everything I did, every choice I made, came down to what African Americans can and can't do, and I was always wrong, never enough. I had been told, implicitly if not explicitly, that African Americans join the African American Awareness Club and choose monologues written by African Americans—*real ones.* Well, I knew one thing, *this* African American doesn't put on a donkey mask and act like an ass in front of the white kids at her school. And for once, this African American was right.

THE SUMMER I LEFT SEWICKLEY

The summer before my senior year in high school, I attended a one-week drama program in Lancaster, Pennsylvania, a four-week pre-college drama program at the University of the Arts in Philadelphia, and a one-week leadership conference in Michigan. I was seventeen and wanted to spend as little time in Sewickley as possible. I thought if I left my small suburban town I'd leave behind the bias and bigotry that resided in it. I was wrong. I went from one white institution to the next. The setting changed but the situation did not.

On day one in Lancaster we were to write a list of ten words that described who we were. "Daughter, sister, student..." stuff like that. We then read our list out loud to the group. After I finished reading my list the teacher—a short, older white man whose face was half hidden behind an unkempt beard, a pair of wire-rimmed glasses, and long brown hair—said, "You know, Melva, I'm surprised you didn't put down African American." My mind went blank. I felt everyone's eyes on me and was at a loss as to what to say.

"It's okay," he said hurriedly, taking in what I can only assume was a worried look on my face. "There's nothing wrong with it," he assured me. "I'm just surprised."

It felt, though, like there *was* something wrong with it. Why hadn't it occurred to me to put African American on my list? I was the only black kid in the class, and it was clear my teacher saw me as such. It was also clear he had a very specific idea of what blackness was. And I wasn't it. That my teacher should care more about what didn't make my list than what did, told me that what he had to say about me was more important than what I had to say about myself.

Everything else on my list was ignored, which is to say, every other part of me was ignored.

The exercise was meant to be an icebreaker, a way for us to get to know one another, but by the end of it I felt like I knew less about myself than I had before. What did it say about me that I should fail to mention such an important part of myself? Why did it feel so wrong? And if my teacher was so surprised by my omission of race, then what else about me—my blackness—might he be surprised by? What part of being African American was I not living up to?

At the pre-college drama program in Philadelphia, I was one of four black kids in the group. My closest friend was Danielle, a pretty Puerto Rican girl from Sarasota, Florida. She drove her own car and complained often about her parents' inability to keep up with the repairs. We both wanted to move to New York after graduation. I thought our friendship had the potential of lasting long after the program ended. But one day, after leaving a casual conversation with the three other black kids in the group, she turned to me and said, "Melva, I'm so glad you don't talk like the rest of them."

I froze. Something inside my head had stopped working. Anyone who says, "You should have said something," doesn't know just how crippling a racist remark can be. It was disarming, really, her honesty, her relief that I should be so unlike the other black kids in our group. I knew then my friendship with Danielle would be short-lived, and I was deeply disappointed by it. I had gained a friend and lost a friend in a matter of weeks. And the reason was rooted in race. I don't think she ever knew how much she hurt me. How could she? I didn't tell her. I couldn't tell her. Her words had silenced me. She, too, had a very specific idea of blackness. And again, I wasn't it. I was the exception. Not the rule. I didn't sound like the black kids. I sounded like the white kids. What then did that say about my blackness? What then did that say about me? One night I sat huddled in a small circle with Danielle and the rest of our group, talking about sex and dating. I kept quiet, having nothing to contribute to the conversation, while the others shared experiences they'd had with their boyfriends and girlfriends. Then, a tall white boy with curly black hair looked across the circle at me and asked, "So, Melva, who has bigger dicks—black guys or white guys?" The rest of the group nodded their head in approval, as if to say "good question." I felt flushed. I didn't know whether to be offended or flattered. For a brief moment, I thought about saying, "Well, I've never seen a white guy's dick but if you'd like to change that...." but didn't have the courage to pull it off. And in truth, I hadn't seen any guy's dick, but it felt foolish to own up to it. Instead I played coy, shrugging it off, as though it was beneath my dignity to answer his question. Of course, he didn't ask any of the other girls that question. He assumed I had been with both black guys and white guys, which I found staggering considering I hadn't been with any guys at all. Maybe it was his way of flirting. Maybe he was testing me to see if I was into white guys. Or maybe it was his way of telling me that a white guy was into me. Still, I was seventeen. I had the sexual experience of a Disney princess. I mean, really, how many dicks did he think I'd seen?

I was one of seven or eight students from my school who attended the leadership conference in Michigan—a misfit group of good to really good students looking to boost their college applications, or at least gain a solid life experience to write about in a college essay. The last night of the conference, a hundred or so students from across the country were separated from the students they came to the conference with and divided into small groups. In my group we talked about race. I mostly listened, very aware that as the only black person in the group, people would be most interested to hear what I had to say. Once everyone had an opportunity to share his or her thoughts, the group leader, a young white woman, turned to me and asked if I had anything to add. I took a deep breath and spoke about how African Americans are judged not as individuals but as a community. Outsiders of the community experience black individuals as representatives of their race. How we speak, how we dress, what we do, and who we are—our family life, social life, professional life, and personal life—all become a reflection, not of the individual, but of the race to which we belong. This means, as an African American, I have to be on my best behavior. I don't have the same second and third chances as my white peers, because my mistakes are associated with the color of my skin.

It just came out. I didn't even have to think about it. It was like I had been waiting for years for someone to ask me about my thoughts on race, and finally someone had. How long had I been holding that in? How long had I felt that I had to be on my best behavior, that when I stepped out the door I was not only representing myself but my community as well? In truth, I still feel this way. I know stepping out of line and speaking out of turn reflects poorly on my race. Therefore, I am who I need to be—a good girl, a nice girl—in order to make those around me more comfortable.

Next, we were to choose one person from the group to stand up in front of everyone else and share what the group had discussed. The group leader nominated me. As I stood before the crowd, I heard my voice waver and felt my body grow tense, and yet I also felt like I was starting to step into myself. This was the person I was meant to be. Someone who wasn't afraid to speak her mind. I was grateful the group leader asked me what I thought, because if she hadn't

I wouldn't have offered my opinion so freely. And I certainly wouldn't have volunteered to stand up and represent the whole group. My hand would have stayed firmly by my side. I would have stayed quiet. Like I always did. I surprised myself that day. I had something to say and didn't even know it.

The lesson I learned that summer, and I'm still grappling with it today, is to not take racism so personally. That's not to say I can't get upset or offended or angry or hurt by it. And it certainly doesn't mean that I ought to ignore it. It means I need to try not to make it about me. I need to work on keeping racism about racists. They're dumping all their shit on me and I'm letting it sink into my skin.

The summer I left Sewickley I internalized every racially tinged remark said to me and about me. I can't do that anymore. I can't afford to. Today, I hold a belief system about myself that has largely been influenced by bigots—that I am not enough. And I am. And if I can't change their way of thinking, then I need to change my own. It's not about me. It's about them.

'I' FOR IGNORANT

When I arrived at NYU I became uncomfortably aware that my peers had very deep thoughts. Deep, compelling, provocative thoughts. Thoughts not only on things but on the *nature* of things. And if that wasn't enough, behind every deep thought was an even deeper need to *share* the thought. In high school, students waited to be called on. They avoided eye contact and slouched in their seats. At NYU, no one was called on. There was no need. Students raised their hands and offered up their opinions freely, eager to share the discoveries they'd made and the lessons they'd learned. I marveled at how "moved" people were by the previous night's reading. Everyone seemed "stirred" or "troubled" by something. *I found the reading subversive. I found the reading dated. I found the reading problematic.* While I, on the other hand, found the reading long, or occasionally, not as long as the night before. Everything was challenged—readings, writings, recordings. I didn't know where I stood on anything. Everyone around me had such a strong point of view. They knew how they felt about people they'd never met, situations they'd never been in, and experiences they'd never had. I knew nothing. Not about anyone or anything—not even myself.

I took rigorous notes in a five-subject bright purple notebook with New York University emblazoned in gold letters. This was my college experience: active listening. Notebooks full of other people's troubling thoughts. I took in what others had to say without nurturing an original thought of my own. It bothered me, of course. It was not what I was there for. I was determined to be a part of the conversation. My academic competitiveness kicked in, and I resolved to be an active participant in class. I did my reading with three different highlighters. I read and waited and read and waited for something to *strike* me. I weaved through words but was left with nothing. Ideas seemed to pop like kernels in everyone else's brain but in mine they were slow and sluggish.

It was the first day of my race and ethnicity class. I was a sophomore. The professor was a black woman with short natural hair. It was a diverse class, and a popular one too, much more so than my classical mythology class. It seemed students at NYU would rather talk about race in the U.S. than the happenings on Mount Olympus.

I took a seat somewhere in the middle. I knew what I had to do—speak early and often. I knew the longer I waited to speak, the harder it would become to do so. And so the first opportunity I got, I took. Introducing myself first, as we were instructed to do, I did what is most encouraged at any collegiate institution and voiced my opinion. Unfortunately…it was the wrong one.

"I don't think there's such a thing as institutionalized racism." Allowing the waves of exasperation to wash over me, I continued, "I think racism exists on a personal level and comes down to the individual at hand. I don't think it's systemic or governed or something that is institutionalized. I think it's something that has to be dealt with on an individual basis." I sat alone. I sat very, very alone, wishing very much that I was on Mount Olympus.

"Does anyone agree with Melva?" the professor asked. The class remained motionless. I willed with all my might someone to raise their hand, to raise their voice, and keep my naïveté at bay. "No one?" the professor pressed on. Was it my imagination or did I detect a note of feigned surprise in her voice? "So, it's just Melva then?" she added with a bit of humor.

I saw heads nodding fervently out of the corner of my

eyes. I sank back into my chair, keeping my eyes low to the ground.

I'm sure there must have been at least one kid who agreed with me, one kid who had never been exposed to institutionalized racism but was too terrified to join my party of one. Hands shot up into the air, and with each retort, it seemed as though I was drifting out to sea. I waited for a life vest from the professor or a classmate that would never come. Clearly she thought more could be learned by letting me drown. It was a slow death. I waited in vain for someone to have my back, to say that my opinion was clearly based only on my life experience, and might it be interesting to know the exactness of those experiences so that we might better understand such a position. It never came.

I regretted what I'd said immediately, not because I found it to be untrue—that wouldn't come for some time—but because of the way it made me feel. Embarrassed and naïve—cut off from the rest of the class, cut off from my community—I couldn't help but take in the disapproving looks. I felt as though a scarlet letter had materialized on my chest: "I" for Ignorant. I had registered for the class to participate in a dialogue, to help solve the problem, and there I was, a part of it.

The class covered everything to do with race: whites thinking they're better than blacks, blacks thinking they're better than blacks, and Beyoncé. Countless conversations left my insides boiling with… What was it exactly? Rage? Fear? Confusion? I couldn't name it, but I'm sure someone else in my class could. After every discussion, the professor would ask if there was anyone who disagreed, thought differently, or could provide an alternative point of view, and a haze of heat would rise from my face. It felt very much like she was speaking directly to me. At once I felt I had nothing to say and so much to say I might burst. *Oh no you don't*, a voice sang inside my head, *We're not going to fall for that again.* Not one word would come out of my mouth after the first class. On Tuesdays and Thursdays from 10:00 a.m. to 11:15 a.m., I remained silent lest I expose an even greater ignorance in me that I didn't know existed.

Today I feel a certain amount of pressure, a certain amount of responsibility, both personally and socially, to be woke and stay woke. I'm careful not to make the same mistake now that I made then. That mistake cost me my confidence and courage. What little of it I had. I'm terrified of saying the wrong thing or asking the wrong question. I keep my hand down and my mouth shut. I think about how much further along my classmates were than I was. How behind I was in the discussion. And I have to wonder if the same is true today. How much more catching up do I have to do? I read articles about race and racism and issues that affect my community, and I take mental notes as if I'm going to be quizzed on it later. It takes work, and admittedly, some days I'm willing to do it and other days I'm not.

The transition from unconsciousness to consciousness is a difficult one. It's uncomfortable. It has to be. How can you know the inner workings of racial inequality and still sit comfortably? You can't. To be woke is to be in a constant state of discomfort. Or so it is for me. That's how I know I'm doing it right. That's how I know I'm getting somewhere. I check my levels of discomfort. My breathing. My heartbeat. Institutionalized racism was too heavy to hold. It made me anxious. I have to commend myself, though, hard as it is, for doing what I did that day. For doing what I set out to do. For putting myself out there. My goal wasn't to be right. My goal was to participate. And that I did. If I can remember that, if I can hold on to that, and not the shame and silence that followed, then maybe I'll be able to do it again. I'll be able to raise my hand, raise my voice, and risk being seen, risk being heard, risk being wrong.

RACIST AF

I was walking back to my dorm one night with three friends from my acting studio: Natalia, Will, and Gabe. I was teasing Gabe. We had done a vocal exercise in class that morning that left him looking utterly ridiculous. Making fun of people wasn't my typical pasttime sport but I thought it harmless and all in good fun. He himself had made light of it earlier that day. I kept reliving his moment of ridicule to the delight of Natalia and Will, laughing along the way. Gabe, however, was not amused. He stopped in his tracks and walked over to me menacingly. Towering over me he said, "Melva, if you don't shut up, I'm going to hang you like they did the other Negroes during the Civil War."

Fucked up: when a white man tells me the precise nature in which he intends to kill me, when his chosen method of murder is inspired by the color of my skin and the historical context it holds, when he uses derogatory language to remind me of a time in history when violence against my race was commonplace, both tolerated and accepted by the masses, even over such things as trivial as teasing a white man.

I stood on the street. Shaken. Scared. I had never been threatened before in my life. It was the first time the color of my skin had been used against me in such a vicious way. It was as if I had temporarily gone back in time and gotten a glimpse into the life I might have lived had I been born during a different era. It was the most racist thing anyone had ever said to me. It still is. I didn't know what to do. I didn't know what to say. It was Natalia who broke the silence. "Wow, Gabe," she said. "You're going to hell."

Gabe and I kept our distance in studio for a short time thereafter, but it wasn't long before things between us were back to normal. My eighteen-year-old self preferred it that way. It was too uncomfortable, painful even, to continually acknowledge the effect his words had had on me by maintaining a strained silence. So I got over it, or seemed to, anyway. I wondered, though, how did he know? How did he know he could get away with it? How did he know I would stay silent?

NOTES FROM THE DIRECTOR

PART TWO: COLLEGE

It was my first audition at NYU. I had chosen to do a comedic monologue from the play *Painting Churches* by Tina Howe. When I finished the piece, the casting director, Alan, a middle-aged white man, gave me a long, inquisitive look, and the following note: *I want you to do it again, and this time I want you to do it as the silliest white girl you know.*

Now it was my turn to look at Alan long and hard and pretend like I knew what he was talking about. I stole a glance at the woman sitting by his side. She was a black woman with dreads draping her long, thin face. She gave a knowing nod and a small smile, and I wondered what it was I wasn't getting. I had no idea how to take the note. First, I thought of a valley girl. They're a little silly, right? Then, I thought of Phoebe from *Friends*. She was definitely silly. Next, I had to wonder how one differentiates between a silly white girl and a silly black girl. And then a new worry—what if I missed the mark completely and portrayed a silly Asian girl instead?

I thought for a moment, and then attempted the monologue again. I raised my voice to a higher pitch and then I contorted my body in a strange fashion, which I was unable to maintain throughout the duration of the piece. I felt like a fool, like I had been called in to entertain the king at court. *Why was this man making me do this?* It was a mess. I thank God it wasn't taped. I had to wonder, though...would he ever give that note to a white actress? To do a monologue like a silly black girl? How might that look? How might that sound?

When I finished the second time, Alan looked at me like

he was working on a puzzle he had no interest in solving and said, "You know, Melva, you're just not funny." Something about his response—his boldness, his bluntness, his boredom—made me burst into laughter. "Okay, thank you for your time," I said politely. As I headed out the door, I caught a glimpse of the black woman sitting by Alan's side and was pleased to see the stony expression on her face. She didn't seem to agree with Alan's assessment of me—a small comfort.

Two years later I found myself under Alan's direction again. I was doing a scene from August Wilson's *Joe Turner's Come and Gone*. One day during rehearsal Alan gave me the following note: *Do it again, and this time before every line, I want you to say, 'Damn, shut up!' or 'Boy, you crazy!'*

I took the note, feeling self-conscious, utterly stupid, and somewhat degraded. My scene partner, who was black as well, was no help to me whatsoever. Every ridiculous note Alan gave him he took without missing a beat. Like stomping his foot, clapping his hands, and shouting "Ooo-eee" or "Mm-mm-mm" before each of his lines. Deep down I was seething. I did not dedicate four years of my life training as an actor at NYU to receive notes rooted in racial stereotypes.

White America has an idea, an image of black people and black American life, and as a black actor I'm asked to support that image and idea in each role I play. And that needs to stop. We need to be in control of our own narrative. We need stories that aren't manipulated. Stories that ring true. White people dictating the story we tell to ourselves and about ourselves is a subtle form of oppression. There are times when I see myself represented on screen or on stage and it's like looking though a funhouse mirror. Yes, there's familiarity there, but also enough distortion to distance myself from the image.

The right to tell my own story, to use my voice, to express

myself, is something I've been fighting for my entire adult life. It's one of the reasons I'm so drawn to the arts to begin with. It's the only place I have the courage to do such a thing. The stage is my one safe and sacred space. When I'm acting I speak my truth. I own my truth. I say what I mean and I mean what I say. Without permission. Without apology. I'll tell you to go fuck yourself without fear of repercussion. I'll tell you I love you without fear of rejection. My power is infinite. I feel capable and in control. I feel heard. I feel seen. I feel understood. But most of all I feel like myself. That day in rehearsal, under Alan's direction, I didn't feel like myself at all. I didn't feel heard. I didn't feel seen. I felt invisible.

THE MISREPRESENTATION OF MELVA GRAHAM

It was against my better judgment, the question I asked, but something made me do it. It was my sophomore year. My scene partner, Robert James, Jr., aloof, distant, bearded, and black, was sitting across from me. He had returned to NYU to finish his training as an actor after leaving a year earlier. I imagine it was difficult for him, joining this close-knit group of people, but if it was, he certainly didn't make it easier on himself. He was reluctant to rehearse outside of class. He was unwilling to participate in group exercises, and when he did, it was only to mention problems with our ideas, never solutions to the tasks we were assigned. When he finally opened up to the class, it was to make fun of those around him. It was as if every day he was hosting somebody's roast. I disliked him the moment I met him. So naturally, I started dating him a year later.

"So, what do people say about me?" I asked.

Rob dropped his gaze and suddenly became interested in the text in front of him—Lorraine Hansberry's *A Raisin in the Sun*. I was playing the part of Beneatha to his Asagai. We were lovers—lovers who challenged one another and made the other think about the world and themselves in a new way. In a few months' time, life would imitate art and I'd spend the next three and half years lying in bed next to him, defending my truth, proving my worth, challenging the arguments he made against me, thinking that was what love looked like—constant combat and some sex here and there. But not yet. Right then I was far from loving him. I had only just begun to tolerate him.

Rob continued to stare at his script. I allowed the silence to settle between us. Rob, feeling the pressure mounting, spoke. "Everyone really looks up to you"—this was where the conversation should have ended—"…for the most part," he added as an afterthought, knowing full well this was the part I would latch on to.

"For the most part?" I repeated back to him.

"There are some…" he hesitated.

"Yes?" I pressed on, wondering what could be on the other side of this sentence.

"There are some who think you're ashamed of being black."

Boom. Something seismic shifted inside of me. I could never have imagined it. It was the most hurtful thing anyone had ever said to me. It still is. Inside I was fuming and from the fumes came fear, knowing that there were words out there that, if strung together properly, could cut me so deeply. It was the first time my sense of self had truly been tested and it failed miserably. I realized the foundation on which it stood—my truth—was no match against the masses. I was dumbfounded. My mind might have made its way back to itself, through the thickets of unbidden thoughts, had it not been so betrayed by my body. It was discomfort unlike anything I had ever known.

"Is it true?" Rob asked tentatively.

"No, it's not," I said defiantly, shifting in my seat. I could feel a large lump inside my chest. It would remain lodged there for the following four days. The stress of it would cause me to consider seeing a doctor. "It's absolutely not." I said again, returning my attention to the material in front of me.

"I hoped it wasn't," he said softly.

Susan, my acting teacher, knew something was wrong the moment I stepped into the room. I loved this about her.

"What is it?" she asked, a look of concern on her face, a Vitamin Water in her hand. "What's happened to you?" I hadn't planned on sharing the truth as to why I had missed class that day and was only now showing up to rehearsal, but the look in her eyes told me she wouldn't have it any other way. I took a deep steadying breath and opened my mouth to speak—

"Not here," she said, rising to her feet. We had the space to ourselves but who knew for how long. The rest of her students would be arriving at any moment. She grabbed me by the wrist and led me out the door and then guided me down the hall and into a secluded darkened stairwell I hadn't known existed. We sat at the top of the stairs, and I told her what Rob had told me.

I didn't just weep. I wailed. I couldn't stop myself. When my sobs subsided, she suggested I go to therapy. I should get curious, she said, as to why this was affecting me so much.

The next day I confided in Tori. She and I were the only black girls in our acting studio. We were close, but not incredibly so. I didn't dare confide in one of my white friends— what if they were in on it too? What if they thought the same? When I told Tori what Rob had told me her expression turned icy and severe. Slowly, she shook her head back and forth. "I'm not surprised," she said heavily. Then she started talking about the kids—the white kids—in our studio. How she once heard so-and-so say this and what's-her-name say that. "I'm not surprised," she said again. I appreciated her candor but was troubled by it all the same. I pictured everyone huddled together talking about how unbelievably un-black I was.

Rob told me there were those who had thought my parents were white. That I must have been adopted. He told me there were those who were surprised to see how moved I was when Denzel Washington and Halle Berry won the Academy

Award for Best Actor and Best Actress. He told me there were those who thought it might be difficult for me to do a piece like Lorraine Hansberry's *A Raisin in the Sun*, a play rooted in the African American experience. He told me all of this, and not once did I think to question him. To confront him. To demand why he didn't stand up for me. This, after all, was an attack on my blackness.

It wouldn't occur to me until much later that Rob might not have been telling me the whole truth. That it might not just have been the thoughts of others but some of his own that he was espousing, but it didn't matter. The damage had been done. He had "inceptioned" me. He planted an idea deep inside my head. An idea I couldn't shake. An idea that would take hold of me and shatter my sense of self. *People think I'm ashamed of being black.* I knew it wasn't true, but it didn't matter. There were those who did. That's what made the idea so debilitating. That's what made it so harsh and hurtful. It didn't matter what I thought. It wasn't up to me. I didn't get a say in what other people thought about me. I didn't have a voice.

Instead of distancing myself from Rob, as I should have done, I distanced myself from the rest of my acting studio and allowed Rob to fill the void. He and I grew closer by the day. Perhaps that's what he intended, what he had hoped for. I knew Rob had a crush on me. What I didn't know was who believed the story he told me (he had refused to name names), and who did not. I could only suspect, and that suspicion was enough to silence me.

We were in rehearsal for *The Love of the Nightingale* by Timberlake Wertenbaker. Inspired by Greek mythology, the play tells the story of Philomele. After her brother-in-law rapes her, he cuts out her tongue so that she is unable to tell anyone. I wanted to play Philomele but instead I was cast as her nanny, Niobe. It was a sizeable supporting role, but still, I wasn't very happy. I was pleased with my performance, though. Susan, my acting teacher and director of the play, told me I was the only one who could have played the part. I received rave reviews from everyone except Rob. While I basked in compliments after the curtain call, Rob looked on in disapproval. He told me he found my performance "problematic."

Susan thought my character should have an accent since she came from a different land than the family she was caring for. I chose to do a West Indian accent, which Rob dubbed as "subversively racist." His argument was that I invoked race into a play that was otherwise colorblind. My use of a black-identified accent brought meaning to the color of my skin and Rob deemed that as racist—subversively so.

I was disturbed and distressed by his criticism. I let it take hold of me and overpower the praise I had been given. I was being accused of being subversively racist. Against whom? My own people? Myself? Subversively racist? What did that even mean? I was bewildered by his response.

He was referring to the West Indian nannies one sees throughout the city pushing strollers across the street. There is a culture of caregivers, particularly caregivers of color, in New York City (one, unbeknownst to me, I would be joining soon) whom I was now commenting on.

So what? I said. So what if I'm commenting on a culture and bringing it to light? This is a culture that is unseen and unheard from, and I'm giving voice to it, was my response. I had an integral part to play in the story, and a beautiful long soliloquy where I spoke about my land and where I came from and how important it was not only to have a voice but to use it… "The silence of the dead can turn into a wild chorus. But the one alive who cannot speak, that one has truly lost all power."[3]

Maybe next time an audience member sees a black woman

---

[3] Wertenbaker, Timberlake. *The Love of the Nightingale*. Woodstock, IL: The Dramatic Publishing Company, 1988. Scene 16, page 51.

hand in hand with two white children on the streets of New York, they won't just see her color or her occupation, they'll see her, they'll hear her story.

Rob didn't buy it. I wondered if anyone else would. I thought about confiding in Tori again but was too afraid of what she might say. So I spoke to a friend from high school instead. We had never talked about race before. I was anxious. I was taking our friendship into unknown territory and was unsure of what I might find. When she sided with me, relief raced through my body, but her support was still not satisfying. She was white. I needed the support of someone who was black. But the only person available to me really was Rob. So I clung to him. Despite the hurt and confusion he had caused me, I clung to him.

Rob was everything I wasn't, and possibly, though it's hard to admit, everything I wanted to be—bold and unapologetically black. If he would accept me for who I was then maybe I could accept myself for who I was. If he would stand up for me then maybe I wouldn't have to stand up for myself. If he used his voice, then maybe I wouldn't have to use my own. But he never did. He challenged me and my blackness as much as anyone else, perhaps even more. I think he knew that when it came to race and identity, the ground on which I stood was so shaky I could fall through the cracks at any given moment, and if he gave me the support I needed, I might stop needing him.

CLASSMATES AND ROOMMATES

I used to share a two-bedroom apartment-style suite on Fourteenth Street between Broadway and Fourth Avenue with two girls who didn't know me and didn't like me. One was white, the other Asian. It was my junior year. The atmosphere in our dorm was tense and at times hostile. I didn't know what I had done to offend them, but I wasn't overly concerned by it. Jessica, my roommate, was spending her spring semester studying abroad in Paris, so I had a room to myself while my suitemates had to share. I suppose they resented that.

They took the initiative to rearrange the furniture in the common living room area and pin up a large floral tapestry that extended itself from one wall to the other, sealing itself off from those making their way to the bathroom or kitchen. It remained closed, except when they hosted a party, had a girls' night, or otherwise occupied the space, and then they'd leave a small opening. I took the hint. They could not have marked their territory more clearly than if they were dogs. Were it forty years earlier, the divisiveness of our living arrangement might have been rooted in prejudice, but due to the struggle and sacrifice of so many, their behavior was rooted in pettiness—that was progress. I took it as a severe slight but didn't let on any sign of it. I thought about staging a sit-in, pulling back the tapestry, and plopping down on the couch with my laptop to enjoy a game of *Snood* but was unable to muster the courage such a confrontation would require. I would have been useless in the sixties. Instead, I continued to silently obey their unspoken rule: *You have your space and we have ours.* All that was missing were signs on the doors and tapestry, pointing us to our designated area, and a fire hose in case I stepped out of line.

Junior year I was the only black girl in my acting studio and not as close to the group as I would have liked. I had my friend, Erin, and boyfriend, Rob, but he acted as a barrier between me and everyone else. My entire identity consisted of being his girlfriend. My classmates saw me through him. They thought I was talented but didn't know me much beyond that. I felt less sure of myself than I ever had in high school. I was full of doubt. I second-guessed what I had to say so much that I said nothing at all. I showed up but I didn't speak up. I was a passive passenger.

One day our acting class had taken a deviation from its regular scene study workshop and were delving into a conversation about politics and production. I stayed silent while Rob made a point I had made to him when discussing the topic in private a few nights prior. He brought up the one thought I had to offer. Did he know what he was doing by stealing my one and only original thought?

"You're the only one who didn't say anything," said Erin, as we walked back to our dorm. I didn't need her to point it out. I felt uncomfortable enough without her shedding light on the subject.

In my theater studies class, we were divided into groups of four to lead classroom discussions which felt impossible. Following through with it seemed unimaginable, but I could see no way out of it. When it was my turn to contribute, I felt as if I'd been placed beneath a microscope. I felt my classmates were judging me harshly and that nothing I said made sense. I wondered how many people heard the trembling in my voice.

The only time I felt like myself was during rehearsal, when I was acting. We were on break one day, and Rob wanted to make it a dance break. He put on his latest jam, then approached me, bopping up and down, swinging back and forth, beckoning me to join him while the rest of the cast watched. I shot him a look of disinterest and backed away. Carly, a petite girl, who liked to show cleavage and make the sound of an orgasm every time she sneezed, chimed in, and provided commentary to the scene unfolding before her. "Melva's like, I don't want to dance, I'm white!" she exclaimed and then laughed uproariously, quite pleased with herself.

I stood on the spot—frozen.

I couldn't believe she had the audacity to call me white to my face—so matter of factly, so self-assured. My heart was pounding inside my chest. I was so furious, I couldn't think. I was so uncomfortable I couldn't speak. Strangely enough, or perhaps not so strange at all, I was just as mad at Rob as I was at Carly. Clever, quick-witted Rob, who could shut someone up with a single word, stood still and watched as I struggled and stuttered.

During my sophomore year I lived with Natalia. One weekend we went shopping with her boyfriend, his best friend, and another girl from our acting studio. Natalia bought a hat along with a pair of large gold hoop earrings. She put them on in the car, crossed her arms, and said, "What's up, nigga?" An electric current coursed through my body. I was both angry and embarrassed. I felt small and insignificant, disrespected by my friend. I wanted to say something, but I didn't want to draw more attention to myself. I didn't want to make a thing of it. I wanted to pretend like it had never happened, and have the moment pass as quickly as possible. It could have been simple. I could have said, "Natalia, please do not use that word in front of me. If you want to be racist behind my back then go ahead, but please don't do it to my face." How easily the words come to me now; I must remember it for next time.

Still, living with Natalia was more bearable than living

with Rachel, my roommate freshman year. Rachel was a staunch conservative from Texas. She decorated our dorm with "Don't Mess with Texas" paraphernalia, which included a popcorn bowl, a woven blanket embellished with the Texas state flag, and other merchandise one might find at the Dallas/Fort Worth International Airport. I imagine they were last minute gifts from a grandmother or longtime family friend just before Rachel boarded.

We spoke on the phone several times over the summer about who we were and who would bring what, but when it came time to meet and move in, something had shifted. When we greeted each other, I thought I saw surprise in her face and then disappointment. I recognized it for what it was. I'd seen it before. The summer I spent attending pre-college programs had prepared me for this. She wasn't expecting me to be black. She assumed I was white.

After her parents left, I heard her crying in the bathroom. I knocked on the door. I went in to comfort her. I gave her a hug. I did what any good roommate would do. But it wasn't enough. She continued to show no interest in me, and I, in turn, showed no interest in her. I had my friends. She had hers. Until one day she didn't. And when that day came she didn't turn to me, as I thought she might, she turned to my friends—my white friends—from my acting studio who came over all the time. They hung out in my dorm, and when they were there I watched Rachel make more of an effort befriending them than she ever had with me. That changed, though. It was as if she woke up one morning and decided she wanted, or perhaps needed, to win me over if she was going to win over my friends. About halfway through the school year, when her best friend from home came to visit, they invited me to dinner and a Broadway show. I declined. I couldn't get past how warm she had been when we first talked on the phone over the summer, and then how cold she had been when we met. And how she embraced every person I invited over to our dorm but distanced herself from me. Her reaching out to me would have been a nice gesture had she done it months earlier but when she finally did it was too little too late.

Rachel made sure to tell me that dinner and the show was her treat, but spending an evening with someone, who after months of living with me had decided to accept me only when it was convenient to her, was not my idea of a treat. Had I not had the friends I had, or had those friends been black instead of white, I doubt any gesture would have been made at all. I was boiling with resentment and wanted nothing to do with her. I used to give people a window when it came to accepting me but that window had closed.

In the past, I thought I had to prove myself to my white classmates and roommates. I had to prove that we were more alike than different. It backfired, though. The moment a white person identifies with me, relates to me, and embraces me, my blackness slips away. It's like they can't hold both. They can't hold my blackness and what they consider to be whiteness. That's why Carly called me white. That's why Natalia used the N word. According to them, I wasn't *really* black.

It is easier to see me as more white than black than to accept that who I am is also blackness. This is what blackness looks like on me. Today, it continues to come up. Like many of us, when I meet new people, when I'm on a job interview, when I have to make a first impression, I feel the pressure to prove myself. So much of that is rooted in race. Not only do I have to prove my worth, I also have to prove my blackness. At times, though it's hard to admit, I catch myself having to prove my proximity to whiteness as well—the school I went to, the neighborhood I grew up in—in the hope that I will be accepted.

If my experiences with classmates and roommates have

taught me anything, it's that not everyone is going to like me. Not everyone is going to accept me. Not everyone is going to respect me. My job is, again, not to take it personally and to make it about them and not about me. I'm still working on that. So much of who I am has been influenced by my experiences with race that when I feel left out, like I don't belong, it's hard to believe that race has nothing to do with it.

Race has everything to do with it.

SPEECHLESS

At the beginning of junior year my former acting teacher, Susan, stopped me in the hallway and told me to sign up for "Diversalogues," a series of conversations about diversity in the arts. The director was someone I should know, she said. I was already taking classes on race, ethnicity, and multiculturalism. I thought that would be no different. And so I signed up. But our group was small, and the smaller the group, the harder it is to hide, and the greater the expectation to participate. I had managed well until the very end, though, when it was announced there would be a showcase, and we were to demonstrate our takeaway from a year's worth of discussions.

I was terrified to speak publicly. It was like a part of my brain was holding another part hostage. My biggest fear was being asked what I thought about something. I immediately drew a blank. The only thought that surfaced was, "Why can't I think of anything to say?" I think it was the fear of saying the wrong thing that prevented me from speaking, and the fear of speaking was what prevented new thoughts from entering my head. I knew if I had something to say, I would be obligated to say it.

The night the showcase was being held I could barely make a sound. I had spent the day lying in bed on vocal rest. My acting studio was in rehearsal for the *Henry VI* trilogy. We were going to perform all three plays in one day. Our production was a little over a week away when I had gotten sick and lost my voice. I'd been given strict instructions not to talk. My throat hurt and my head ached. I couldn't breathe through my nose, and when I opened my mouth to speak, I sounded like a dying bird. I could hardly believe my luck. I was told whispering would only make it worse, so I made sure to do plenty of it. I was told to drink hot water with honey and lemon, so I stuck to soda instead. I was told to gargle a few times a day and get plenty of rest. I didn't. Tomorrow, I'd take better care of myself, I'd have to, but that day I was off the hook. "Diversalogues: A Conversation About Race" would have to go on without me. And I couldn't have been happier.

A mound of balled-up tissues and cough drop wrappers littered the space beneath my bed. The solitude I had been craving hours earlier, when I felt my cold coming on, the scratching at the back of my throat, the touch of dizziness, had now been replaced with a deep longing for care and company. I called my parents. Mom answered. I opened my mouth to speak but nothing came out.

I wanted to discuss the showcase. I wanted to tell her how unhappy I was and how worthless I felt. Even if I had been well, I still wouldn't have wanted to go. I had nothing to offer, nothing to contribute, nothing to say. I wanted her to tell me it was okay that I didn't want to stand up and speak out in front of strangers about my experience with race and racism, but I was afraid she'd try to persuade me to do otherwise. Deep down she'd have known it was what I really wanted to do. It was who I wanted to be. Someone who confronted her discomfort. Someone who stood up and faced her fear. Someone who spoke the fuck up and didn't hide behind a head cold. Instead, I said nothing. It's what I was good at.

That night, I decided to show up to the diversity showcase sick rather than to call in sick. It would look better. Plus, I could no longer stand the solitary confinement of my bedroom. I was also curious. I wanted to hear the conversation about race led by my peers. I took a seat in the audience near the back, clutching a wad of tissues and sucking on a cough drop. The director of the "Diversalogues" series asked if I had something to share. Perhaps something written that someone else could read? *Shit. Didn't think about that.* I shook my head "no" and mouthed the word "sorry." Then I fixed my face to match the look of disappointment on his. The lights dimmed. The audience applauded. The showcase began. I was thankful I was unable to take part in it. The pressure that had been mounting for weeks was now off and a huge weight had been lifted from my chest. Still, I couldn't help but imagine myself behind the podium, microphone in hand, and wonder what I might have said—if I had a voice.

I realize the extent to which race and identity informed my insecurity, and how that insecurity cut off my connection and communication to the rest of the world. If I was to find and use my voice, I had to reconcile my relationship with race. Repair it. Reclaim it. I had been silenced and shamed so many times I was now starting to silence and shame myself. The parts of me that remained strong and secure I didn't dare share with anyone lest they damage that part of me, too—intentionally or not—and I'd be left with nothing, a shell of my former self.

As I watched my peers at the showcase that night, I remembered the week I'd spent at the leadership conference in Michigan and how I had stood in front of all those people and given my perspective on race. I wondered where that girl was now, the one who stood and spoke so freely and openly. It was as if we'd never met before.

When I left home to go to college, I thought I would become the person I was meant to be. I had so much to say, and I thought I'd finally be able to, encouraged to, say it. I thought I would become as fierce off stage as I was on stage, but instead of finding my voice, I lost it.

NOTES FROM THE DIRECTOR

PART THREE: POST-COLLEGE

In my first play after graduation I was cast as Helena in Shakespeare's *A Midsummer Night's Dream*. Richard, the director of the play, was a bald middle-aged white man and former teacher of mine at NYU. At the end of rehearsal one day, while giving notes to the cast, he shared with me his vision of Helena. "I imagine her," he began in his thick British accent, "as one of those big loud women you see on the A train." There was but one word missing from that sentence and it couldn't have been clearer. Black. He was referring to black women.

The A train stops at Columbus Circle, a few blocks away from Lincoln Center, where we rehearsed. The next stop on the A train after Columbus Circle, going uptown, is 125th Street—Harlem. Harlem is less than twenty percent white and more than sixty percent black. It's a stop where a lot of black people get on and off. Richard didn't say one of those big loud women you see on the subway. He said the A train. The A train is race specific. "Big" and "loud" is also how black women have been portrayed in film and on TV for years. Historically, it's how we've been characterized. This is what coded language sounds like.

My heart skipped a beat.

So that's how you see Shakespeare's Helena? As a big loud woman who rides the A train? Have you always seen Shakespeare's heroine as such, or was it only recently, after you cast a black actress in the role? I expect if I had been cast as Titania or Hermia my note would have been the same. I suppose he wanted me to roll my neck and wave my finger and say Shakespeare's iambic pentameter with sass and attitude. But that's not who I was and it was not who I was going to be. It did not match my vision of Helena at all. When you're acting you're supposed to bring yourself into the role. Acting is about honesty and authenticity, it's not a put-on act; it's an experience you live through truthfully.

Richard went on to say the production was an educational tour and we would be performing for a lot of schools from diverse backgrounds, and this was what they would be expecting to see from me. Translation: black kids. We're going to be performing for a lot of black kids.

"I disagree," I told him. My words were clear if not altogether strong. Short, but loaded with meaning. If it were true that we would be performing for a lot of black kids, I thought my presence on stage would be more than enough for them. How could they be expecting a particular performance from me when I doubt they would be expecting me at all?

I didn't think putting on some sort of modern-day minstrel show, which is exactly what he was asking me to do, was what they expected to see, and if they were expecting it, I certainly wasn't going to give it to them. I was going to raise their expectations a bit higher. And how the hell could a middle-aged white man from England know what black kids from New York were expecting from me anyway?

My conversation with Richard had sucked all the life out of me. I was exhausted when I returned home. Proud though I was for openly contradicting him instead of nodding my head in agreement, I was disheartened that I should have to do so in the first place. It occurred to me that in the past I had remained silent. *Yes, I must remember that.* I had allowed directors to give me notes based on my race instead of my role. But I didn't do it that day. I stood up for myself. Could that be growth? Is that why I felt so uncomfortable? As I began to find my voice, I also began to lose my nerve. I don't think I even looked at my script that night. Instead, I collapsed on my couch and cried.

I encountered two young black girls during the run of the show. The first gave me a very strange look when I told her I was playing Helena. And I knew I had been right. The young girl was surprised to see me, someone who looked like her, in the role. The second young girl I encountered reminded me so much of myself I felt my heart lift and break at the same time. How's that possible? We were doing a talk-back after one of our shows. A white woman raised her hand and then took the microphone that was being passed around.

"We," the woman said, with a nod to the young black girl by her side, "have a question for Melva." The young girl looked on in silence as the woman next to her continued to speak. "How long have you been acting?"

I directed my answer to the young girl since I knew it was she who wanted to know. "I started when I was very young," I said. "Probably around your age. I did school plays and I took acting classes. And then I went to college to study acting, too."

The young girl smiled. The woman next to her said thank you, and the microphone was passed on to someone else.

At another talk-back, a young white man asked if there was a specific intention behind the casting of my character, Helena, and that of Hermia. He said Helena is traditionally depicted as having fairer skin than Hermia. Was doing the opposite deliberate? In other words, he wanted to know why a black woman was playing a traditionally white role. Or, at least, that's how I interpreted his question. I spoke up first. Looking back, I'm surprised I did. I told him the only real significant depiction of the characters is the difference in height. Helena is tall and Hermia is short, which I and the other actress were. There's an entire scene where Helena makes fun of Hermia's size and Hermia does the same to Helena. Fair skin, on the other hand, has no real relevance in the play. The young man who asked the question didn't have a response. No one else spoke on the matter. My answer seemed to be sufficient.

I realize now, though, that it was white people, like that young man, and not, as Richard had said, black kids who expected to see a certain performance from me. If a black actress was going to do Shakespeare then she must give a stereotypical black performance in order to justify the casting. Right? She has to be big and loud. Otherwise, what's the point?

Today, I hold on to my resistance, as small as it may seem. Richard, like other white directors I worked with, had tried to reduce me to the color of my skin and the connotations it held. But I didn't let him. I also hold on to the young black girl who was too timid to ask her own question. Her shyness. Her silence. Her not wanting to draw attention to herself. That's me. Or at least, it used to be.

THE GIRL WHO DIDN'T GET THE MEMO

I ran into an old friend at an audition. Her name was Christine. She and I had done a summer study abroad program together in Amsterdam for eight weeks while in college. It had been a few years since I had last seen her. She stood in a crowd of eager actors signing their names to the non-union sheet hoping to be seen. She was the only white actor present. Everyone else was black. This was an open call for *Seven Guitars*, the fifth play in August Wilson's *Century Cycle*. I couldn't help but wonder what Christine was doing there but tried my best to be polite about it.

After we had finished catching up on our latest happenings since graduation, she took a moment and then said, "So...is this, like, a black play?"

"Well, it's August Wilson," I said.

"Oh. Right..." she said, a little unsure of herself.

How could she have gone through four years of training at NYU's Tisch School of the Arts and not know that August Wilson, one of the greatest American playwrights, chronicles black American life throughout the 1900s, one play for each decade? I know who Arthur Miller is. I know who Tennessee Williams is. I know who Eugene O'Neill is. Why didn't she know who August Wilson was?

"Do you think the director would mind seeing me? I mean every audition is an opportunity, right?"

"Yeah, definitely. I mean, they might keep you in mind for another show they're doing this season." Sometimes I'm too polite for my own good.

"Yeah," she said. "I just don't want to be the girl who didn't get the memo."

"Yeah, well, you kind of *are* that girl," I said, unapologetically, pleased at my own directness.

"Yeah...I think I'm going to stay," she said, after giving it some thought. "I think I'm going to audition. I mean I'm already here."

"Yeah," I said. "You never know."

I didn't allow myself to feel the anger and resentment I'm feeling now. I pushed it aside, as I always do. Still, I couldn't believe I was making a white actor feel more comfortable about auditioning for a black play. I don't know what offended me most, the fact that she didn't know who August Wilson was to begin with, or the fact that after finding out who he was, she chose to audition for his play anyway, showing a complete disregard and lack of respect for him and his body of work, as well as the people his work was meant for.

I remember auditioning for a production of *The Laramie Project* by Moisés Kaufman. On my way to the audition my college boyfriend, Rob, said, "Do you really think they're going to cast you? The play takes place in Wyoming. How many black people do you think live in Wyoming?" What kind of shitty thing is that to say to your girlfriend on her way to an audition? I didn't argue with him though. I was too defeated. According to Rob, *The Laramie Project* was a white play. But I showed up anyway. When I arrived at the audition location I was one of two black people sitting in the holding room area. Everyone else was white.

Was I Christine? Was I the girl who didn't get the memo? Was I showing up to places where I didn't belong? No. *Seven Guitars* is different. *Seven Guitars* is a race-specific play. *The Laramie Project* is not. Race is not an issue. It doesn't come up. Who cares if the black population of Laramie, Wyoming, is under two percent? Who cares? One day—one fine day—I'll go to Wyoming. I'll find the one black family who lives in Laramie. I'll sit down and I'll hear their story. But until then....

Both Christine and I were able to audition for *Seven Guitars* that day.

She didn't get the part, though.

But then again, neither did I.

PART TWO

THE 'S' WORD

Sophie Lindsay Carter Cooper had been on this earth for three and a half years and already she was over it. Everything was stupid. The midtown Manhattan luxury apartment she resided in was stupid. The synagogue where she attended preschool three half-days a week was stupid. Snack time, bath time, and bedtime were stupid. And I, her nanny, was stupid.

"Don't take it personally," her mother, Laura, sighed, as a door slammed shut somewhere in the distance. Sophie had retreated to her room but not before throwing me a dirty look. "She calls me stupid almost every day." Laura shrugged. This, of course, was true, as I soon learned, and though it was somewhat a relief to know I was in good company, it didn't make me feel better. How often do we take personally the very thing we have been advised not to?

Laura waved her hand as though it was nothing, but I thought I detected a trace of sadness in her voice. I couldn't blame her. If Sophie was a pistol, words were her ammunition. Words like, "Go away, stupid" or "I hate you, stupid" or "You're stupid," were loaded into her arsenal, and her mother stood directly in the line of fire.

I had been in their household for less than ten minutes and already had wounds to tend to—old ones that had been reopened and new ones that needed to be patched up.

It seems impossible now that I spent an entire afternoon with that child and walked away unscathed, but I had managed to do so when I interviewed for the position. Sophie showed no signs of malcontent that day. Instead she was quiet and still, not altogether shy, but reserved.

It was mid-December and I was preparing to go home for

the holidays. I had just celebrated my twenty-third birthday and was approaching the end of my first year out of college. I arrived to my interview desperate to secure a steady income before returning home to face my family and friends.

Somehow Sophie seemed to know this about me. Sitting on her mother's lap, she surveyed me with polite curiosity, as though she could read my thoughts and was making her mind up about me.

"Would you like to show Melva your room?" Laura asked her daughter. Sophie considered the question for a moment and then hopped down from her mother's lap and extended an open hand to me. I took it graciously. She took me on a tour of their home and then introduced me to her stuffed animals and pet fish. When I left, she offered me a very sparkly sticker—the three-year-old sign of approval, which, on my first day, seemed to have been revoked.

I ran over the kids' daily routine in my head while Laura rambled on. My first day was proving to be more challenging than I had anticipated.

"It took her a long time to start talking, you know," Laura went on to say. "We thought something was wrong. She was always nodding and shaking her head, pointing and grunting." Laura laughed. "Only Ben seemed to understand what she was saying." Laura took a moment to ponder the interpretation skills of her six-year-old son. "Then she started speaking and seemed to have so much to say." Laura breathed a sigh of relief. There might have been a tear in her eye. "We were so happy. I think she was getting annoyed at having to have someone else speak for her," she said.

Laura peeked down the hallway, straining her ears for sounds of movement. "Maybe she's gone back to sleep," she whispered hopefully. "She needs more rest. She's been waking up at five for over a week now." As Laura's wish became my own, the sound of a door opening and feet stomping could be heard in the background. Sophie returned with blotches of pink on her cheeks and tears sparkling in her eyes, her hair tangled and matted, her long nightgown twisted and wrinkled. She seemed to be coming undone. Laura deflated at the sight of her daughter, wide-eyed and woebegone.

"Feeling better?" she asked.

"No!" Sophie answered back.

I could have told her that, I thought to myself.

"Did you have enough breakfast?" Laura asked gently.

Sophie shot her mother a look of disdain, as though breakfast was beneath her, and then turned her attention on to me. "You get out of here!" she said, in her dry monotonous voice.

"But I like it here," I said, hoping she would match my enthusiasm. And it was true, I did like it there—the apartment was like something out of *Architectural Digest*. "And I can't wait for us to play with all your toys and games," I continued in a sing-song voice, taking on the "this is just going to be a fun playdate so your mom can do whatever she does" approach. "We can bake cookies. Or build a fort. Or have a dance party." I threw my voice up into the air, making each activity pop. "We can play dress up. Or do an art project. Or—"

"Stop talking to me," Sophie snapped. And I obeyed. We stared at one another for a moment, sizing each other up.

"That's not very nice," I said in a sad voice, frowning to gain sympathy. Sophie looked at me in disgust and then turned to her mother for help.

"Get her out of here," she demanded, bouncing on the balls of her feet as if gearing up for a boxing match.

"Aw, Sophie, you're making Melva sad," Laura said, drifting off into the entryway.

I exaggerated my face even more, looking and feeling utterly put out.

"I hate her," Sophie said.

"No you don't," Laura snapped, rejoining us in the family room, bundled up in a long winter coat, scarf and gloves in hand.

"Yes I do," Sophie said, matter of factly. "She's stupid." Laura ignored this most recent attack on my intelligence. "Well…" she said awkwardly, and then decidedly, "I'm off!" Laura snatched up her purse and made to run out the front door. Sophie screamed and latched herself to her mother's coat as though she were a magnet. I stood frozen, unsure of what to say or do next. Laura's abrupt departure had thrown me. I wracked my brain for more questions to ask, but she seemed to have covered everything—except discipline, that is. Then I realized, when it came to discipline, Laura probably had fewer suggestions on the matter than I did.

Sophie grabbed some of the fringe from her mother's scarf and yanked hard on it. Laura choked, coughed, and then regained herself, shooing Sophie away with her purse. She fought her way out the door and into the hallway, her daughter trailing behind her, tugging on her coat, crying and screaming. Sophie raced her mother to the elevator, her arms outstretched as if determined to fling her body in front of the doors to create a blockade, but Laura got there first. She stiff-armed Sophie while holding down the elevator button with her free hand, all with a smile. "I know, I know," she said soothingly but sternly, "but you need time to get to know your new friend, Melva."

"She's *not* my friend! I don't like her!" Sophie protested, stomping her foot.

"Yes, you do," Laura responded, catching her breath.

"No, I don't!" Sophie kicked her mother in the shin.

"Ouch!" Laura cried out, as the elevator doors opened, and she rushed inside with a limp, again warding Sophie off with her purse. "You behave yourself!" Laura scolded. Sophie gave one final roar.

"Mommy always comes back," Laura said, as though she had once considered otherwise. "She always comes back." As the doors closed shut, Laura managed a feeble, "Thank you, Melva," and then was gone.

It was just Sophie and me in the hallway. The finality of the elevator doors closing, the faint sound of its movement passing the floors beneath it, meant the end of the battle, and Sophie had lost. I couldn't tell if the resounding *ding* of the elevator's departure signified the end of round one or the beginning of round two—glass half empty, glass half full. Sophie looked at me as if to say, "You did this!" She balled her fists and began breathing hard, panting almost. Were she a cartoon character, steam would be fuming from her nostrils and ears. I approached her the same way I would a stray dog, lovingly but with caution. In the end, I had to pick her up, my arms outstretched, maintaining a safe distance between us. She fought me the entire way, pinching and kicking any part of me she could reach.

A door opened at the end of the hall. An elderly woman wearing a nightgown peeked her head out and reviewed the scene before her: me wrestling a three-year-old child back into her home as she hollered and squirmed in protest. The woman's face was impassive, she stared at the child struggling against her will and then sniffed loudly—she could have been Sophie eighty years from now.

Once inside I made the mistake of bending down to Sophie's level to try to reason with her. She punched me in the arm and then took off at a run toward her bedroom, mumbling, "Stupid, stupid, stupid!" before slamming the door shut and falling back to sleep—fulfilling her mother's wish after all.

Sophie liked to assign new meaning to words and construct sentences that made sense only to her. I don't suppose it worried Laura too much. Her verbal skills, though unique, showcased a high aptitude for one her age. And though her words at times were meaningless and her sentences nonsensical, she always spoke with a sly grin on her face that seemed to suggest she knew exactly what she was up to. She had a nickname for everyone, words that were most commonly found in the pantry, like cookie or pepper or chip. She'd greet her fellow classmates at the Central Park Zoo with "Hello, Cheerios!" then stifle a giggle that was all to herself. The other children would take offense at this and then come to me for a solution. I'd say that Sophie didn't mean anything by it, that's just her way of showing affection. "No, it's not," she'd say out of the side of her mouth.

She had a slew of catch phrases she'd picked up like a child star on a 90s sitcom, cueing up the laugh track with "Get a grip!" or "Not my problem!" and finally, "You're not the boss of me!" Though not as verbal as her older brother, Ben, Sophie was conversational when she wanted to be. Her voice was raspy and low, a good octave or two below her brother's, and though her words were sparse, they were delivered in a tone that seemed to say, "This is as good as it gets." I'd often imagine her sneaking out of bed and into a speakeasy down the street to blow off steam and throw back a few.

Despite being petite, Sophie was as physically threatening as she was verbally. No matter what position she happened to be in, whether standing up, siting down, or lying on her bed, Sophie could almost always be found kicking and punching the air. It was as though a punching bag only she could see was constantly swinging and swaying before her. When her feet or fists made contact with another person, she'd grin mischievously, then aim at her target again. I'd sometimes catch her tapping her thumb and forefinger together absent-mindedly while I read to her, as though practicing her pinching, ready to strike as soon as the situation called for it.

She had an incredible amount of strength for one so small, a strength she liked to show off at the grocery store by picking up two bags at once and throwing them over her shoulder. She'd lead the way through the sliding glass doors, then down the street, stopping at the corner, where she'd set the bags down, panting slightly, and then shoot her hand up into the air to hail a cab. When she'd catch me doing the same, she'd scrunch up her face and say through gritted teeth, "Stop copying me."

And though the streets of Manhattan were long and most of her activities were too close to cab it, Sophie had no further use for a stroller. She had done away with the thing a few months prior and now regarded anyone in use of one with contempt.

"She's too big to be in a stroller," she'd shout, pointing directly into a little girl's face as we walked down Third Avenue together. "He doesn't need a stroller either!" she scolded, as a sleeping toddler rolled along past us. "And why are they using a stroller?" she cried out indignantly, as two children, one far bigger than the other, wheeled on by, looks of bored smugness on their faces. She must have been tired herself. We'd walked several blocks and had a few more to go, but she'd never own up to it. Unwilling to walk hand in hand with me, she pulled the part of my sleeve she was clinging to, demanding answers. I explained how babies needed strollers, and she muttered in response, "Those weren't babies," and then continued along her way, an unmistakable look of superiority etched across her face (#StrollerShaming).

I thought each day would be my last. Laura seemed to share this notion. Afraid, no doubt, that her daughter's name calling would get to me, as it certainly was, and send me out the door, she worked tirelessly to reassure me of how happy they all were to have me as their nanny. "The kids just love you. They really adore you. We all do. You're just so wonderful." Then Sophie would shoot me a stink-eye from across the room and ask for their previous nanny, a woman with two young children of her own, who was fired when she told the kids she loved them more than their parents. That would not be a problem for me, I thought to myself. The most I could do was love them like an estranged aunt who doesn't call or send money on birthdays.

I tried discipline, of course—demanding an apology, giving her a time out, sending her to her room, taking away privileges—but it didn't matter. Nothing matters when everything's stupid. What did she care if she missed an episode of *Sponge Bob*? They show reruns all the time. Or if she wasn't getting any dessert that night? She knew what ice cream tasted like.

Calling me stupid was so entwined with her personality, on days when the name-calling was lacking I worried she might be getting sick. At night I'd go into her room after bedtime to check and see if she was still breathing and would catch her mumbling in her sleep, "stu...pid...stu...pid...stupid." It was as if her subconscious knew I had entered the room.

In the end I grew accustomed to it and even began to tolerate it. I had no other choice really. I had sustained so many injuries to my ego, it seemed to have withered up and died.

Then one day it stopped. It was as if she had never known the word, as though it had been wiped clean from her vocabulary. There were weeks, several golden weeks, when a sudden transformation had taken place, and I seemed to have won her over at last. She resorted to Melvie, or Melvs, when addressing me. I have to say, out of all the nicknames I have been given, no one before or after Sophie would call me Melvs—that was all her own. Perhaps it was that which signified the growth in our relationship. Laura remarked on how grown-up Sophie sounded. Like a college student, she said. It was like the past few months had never happened. And I could finally breathe a deep sigh of relief.

And then a new name replaced the old.

I couldn't tell you the circumstance in which it was introduced. I remember the delivery though, casual and offhand, a throw-away line, meaningless and empty, but the words on either end of it are now missing from my memory. We could have been on our way to a playdate, building blocks, or baking cookies. We could have been having pancakes at EJ's, the diner across the street from ballet, or walking home from a piano lesson. I remember I asked her to repeat herself, in case I had misheard. The word had sent a shockwave down my spine and my heart had given a sudden jolt.

"What did you say, Sophie?"

"I said, come on, *snicker*."

Snicker.

That's what I thought she said.

"Uh, yeah, that little girl is calling you nigger." My college boyfriend, Rob—aloof, distant, bearded, and black—was playing Madden Football on the Xbox I'd bought him two Christmases earlier. "If it sounds like nigger and it feels like nigger, then guess what!" Rob placed his eyes on me for the first time in what felt like thirty minutes. "She calling you nigger. Defense! Goddammit!"

Something burned inside my chest. My small studio apartment suddenly seemed overcrowded with Rob, Sophie, Madden, me, stupid, snicker, stupid, snicker. I opened the windows to get some fresh air.

"There you go! There you go! Touchdown!" Rob leapt up from the couch and began to do a little jig. His eyes lit up and he grinned from ear to ear. He wrapped one arm around me and gave me a rough wet kiss on the side of my face. "Come on now, give me some sugar, sugar!" he said, altering his voice to a deep, low grumble, as if there was phlegm stuck in his throat.

"Ew!" I snapped back at him, pulling away. "Don't do that," I said. Rob busted out laughing. "You know I hate that!" I continued, as Rob laughed obnoxiously at himself. "Don't kiss me while doing that voice. It's disgusting," I said, wiping the side of my face with the palm of my hand.

Rob returned to his jig and continued to cackle. I had a sudden urge to yank the plug to his Xbox from its socket and fling the whole thing out the window. Then he caught my eye and looked at me as though he was just now seeing me for the first time, as if I had just gotten home. "What's wrong?" he asked uncertainly.

"Are you kidding me right now?" I glared at him. "What's wrong? Oh, I don't know, let's see, a three-year-old called me nigger today, so you know, that kinda sucked."

I turned on him and stormed off, taking all of two steps, unsure of where I was headed, before he caught me by the arm and turned me back around. "Okay, look, why don't you just tell the mom...what's her name?"

"*Laura*," I said emphatically. I had been saying her name ten times a day, every day for weeks.

"Why don't you just tell Laura that her daughter...what's her name?"

"*Sophie!*"

"Sophie called you a nigger today," he said matter of factly. It wasn't a suggestion. It was bait. And my job was to struggle not to bite. Rob was testing me. He loved to test me in moments of distress. He wanted a debate about race, but first he had to find a way in and that was it.

I stood silent for a moment, unsure of which turn to take, and then finally gave in. "So you think that's what she meant when she called me snicker?"

"That's what you said."

"No, it's not. That's what *you* said. *I* said she called me snicker and it sounded like and felt like she was calling me nigger."

"So then she was calling you nigger."

"No, I don't know that. I have no idea what a snicker is, I only know—"

"What it sounded like and felt like. Yeah, I know." Rob had resumed his game.

"So do you think she was calling me nigger or not?"

"Why does it matter what I think?"

"Oh, dear God! You are so infuriating!"

"Look!" he said loudly, his temper rising to match mine. "It doesn't matter what I think or not, I'm not the one she called nigger." I wanted to take a page out of Sophie's book and punch him in the arm. I knew my anger was misdirected, but I didn't care. In that moment Rob seemed to have earned my fury and frustration just as much as Sophie had. "I told you. Call up the mom, tell her what her daughter called you, and tell her how it felt. Here, you can use my phone. What's the number? I'll dial."

That was the other thing about Rob. When faced with a problem, he loved to make suggestions he knew I wouldn't take. It was his way of calling me a coward. "Forget it," I said and then went into the bathroom to take a long hot shower. When I got out Rob had abandoned his video game and was now typing away on my computer.

"Were you crying in there?" he said, his eyes glued to the screen in front of him. "You were in there for a very long time."

I took a steadying breath. "Yes," I said, deciding there was no need to lie. "Yes, I was."

Rob gave a low noncommittal grunt.

I returned to the bathroom to put on my pajamas. I suddenly did not feel comfortable dressing in front of him. As I slid into bed that night, a small voice inside my head asked, "Why are we keeping him around again?" To which I had no reply.

Sophie called me snicker the following day. And the day after that. And the day after that. And the day after that. I never thought I'd miss being called stupid. Now that snicker seemed to have permanently replaced it, I longed for it almost as much as my real name. There were times when she used the word out of hostility—when she didn't get her way, or was made to do something she didn't want to do—I knew her intention was to hurt me—but other times it was said kindly and with care.

Want to play a game, snicker?

When will mommy be home, snicker?

Can I have more macaroni and cheese please, snicker?

That troubled me most of all. It made me feel like I was her pet. Like my sole purpose in life was to tend to her, play with her, feed, bathe, clothe, and take care of her. The thought of it intensified with each passing day. My spirit sank to a place it would not return from. Was this her image of me? Was I her pet? I did follow her everywhere she went. Always one or two paces behind, I kept up with her with a slow but deliberate trot. Sometimes there was the need to break out into a full run and chase after her. Could it be that on our trips to the park or playground she thought she was taking *me* on a walk? That *I* was the one who needed the exercise and fresh air and not the other way around? *Was I her pet snicker?* And the barometer of whether I was a good snicker or a bad one depended on the day and was measured by her mood.

It's frightening when you realize a word is more powerful than you are. It lets you know you have a lot of work left to do on yourself and where you stand in the world. The use of one two-syllable, seven-letter word and suddenly I was reduced to nothing. It was remarkable, really. How someone so small in size could make me feel so small in stature.

Meanwhile, Sophie and Ben's dad, Mark, was leaving

articles for me to read written by black conservatives and trying to convince me that privatizing social security was a good idea. He'd mention the support of politicians and pundits I had never heard of and then say, "He's an African American Republican." I wanted to tell him I didn't give a flying fuckity fuck about anything he had to say, particularly when his daughter refused to call me by my name.

Laura came to my rescue one day. "Mark dear, Melva has parents of her own, who I am sure convey to her the importance of politics." Only then did he back down. When he left Laura and me alone in the kitchen, she whispered to me, "Don't mind him," and then added secretively, "I voted for Kerry."

Laura came home early one afternoon in distress. She'd had a run-in earlier that day with a woman she hadn't seen in decades. I sat down at the kitchen counter to listen. Sophie was watching *Sponge Bob* and Ben was on the school bus heading home. The woman Laura spoke of was black and had entered Laura's childhood school. It was clear that Laura was speaking around the issue. It was also clear that she needed me to validate whatever thoughts and feelings she was having. What I discerned from the conversation was that Laura hadn't made it easy for that black woman to acclimate herself to a new and predominantly white school, and Laura was feeling somewhat guilty about it. "I mean, she wanted to be a Jewish white girl and she just wasn't," she blurted out. "I don't know, what do you think, Melva?"

I think she wanted to have friends and be included at a new school but you wouldn't offer that to her because she looked different than you.

Her story reminded me of that day in reading circle. In an attempt to answer her question, I began to tell Laura what happened to me that day in first grade. I hadn't spoken of the incident for years and was not quite sure why I had chosen that woman and that moment to do so. Laura listened while putting away groceries. When I finished, she heaved a deep sigh and said, "Every mother's nightmare."

I wasn't sure what she meant by it. Was it every mother's nightmare that her child has something racist said to her? Or every mother's nightmare that her child might say something racist to another child?

The buzzer rang. It was the doorman signaling that Ben had arrived in the lobby, having been dropped off by the school bus.

"Will you go and meet him?" Laura asked, as though I hadn't just shared a deep and personal moment in my life.

"Oh, yeah, of course," I jumped up and made my way out the door, feeling vulnerable and exposed.

I was leaving town for a few days and my friend Katie was going to fill in for me. I was a little nervous, unsure of what torment Sophie might subject her to.

"I want you two to be on your best behavior. Katie is super fun and super nice," I said to Ben and Sophie as they sat at the kitchen counter eating dinner. Laura looked on, nodding in agreement.

"Melvie?" Ben piped up.

"Yes, Ben."

"What color skin does Katie have?"

I bristled. "Uh, well, the same color skin as you, Ben." It felt strange to say white skin so I avoided it as best I could.

"Oh," he said, a bit surprised, before diving into his dinner.

"Why do you ask that, Ben?" asked Laura. That was bold. I was afraid of hearing what was on the other end of the question but Laura trudged on, unafraid of what her six-year-old son might say.

"Well, because people with white skin are more likely to have a BlackBerry than people with dark skin."

Ben was a cell phone junkie. He knew what kind of phone everyone in his life had along with their network provider.

Laura and I shared a brief moment of silence. Sophie continued shoving food into her mouth. It was clear Laura didn't know how to respond to her son, so I took the reins. "Well, you know, Ben," I began. "My parents both have a BlackBerry and so do my aunt and uncle." None of that was true. Soon every black person I knew would carry a BlackBerry. "It may just be that you know more people with your color skin than mine, so it seems like more people with your color skin own a BlackBerry. You just need to meet more people with my color skin." Why was it so difficult to say black or white?

"Oh," Ben said thoughtfully, before returning to his meal.

I gathered my belongings and said my goodbyes.

"I hope what Ben said didn't offend you?" asked Laura.

"Oh no, not at all," I lied. I wondered what it might be like to answer honestly. Instead I stayed silent, brushed it aside, and made my way out the door.

The following week I returned to work hoping that in my absence Sophie might have forgotten my nickname. She hadn't.

"Did that three-year-old call you nigger today?" Rob continued to be unsupportive, making matters worse for me.

"No," I lied. He looked at me.

"Yeah, she did," he said, his eyes staring into mine. "You're such a bad liar," he said with a smile, and then returned to his game of Madden. "I think you're embarrassed by it, Mel. Are you embarrassed by it?"

I ignored this. "How's your team doing, babe?"

Rob grimaced. The Redskins were losing. Again. "Never mind," he said. "We don't have to talk about it."

It was hard to admit at the time, but Rob had been right. I *was* embarrassed, but I felt like admitting it meant owning up to some deep-rooted shame, and I was unable to do that. My biggest worry was being confronted with that shame in public. I feared Sophie might say it at school when I picked her up or on a playdate when I dropped her off. ("Hello, snicker." "Goodbye, snicker." "What took you so long? I've been waiting, snicker.")

I didn't know what I might do or say if I had to deal with that embarrassment in front of others. I imagined their scrutiny. Their intense gaze upon me. And their thoughts so loud I could have answered back to them. *What did that little girl just call her nanny? It sounded a lot like she was calling her the N word. Oh, how awful. I wonder how she's going to handle this. I'm going to stop what I'm doing and watch.* Every time I stepped outside with Sophie, I held my breath.

I asked her repeatedly what the word meant but instead of an answer she'd give me a sly grin and a look that said, *Oh, you know what it means.*

I couldn't help but feel like she was calling me nigger, not just because of Rob's insistence, but because that had been my gut reaction upon hearing the word myself. I felt like snicker was the playground word for nigger, in the same way heck is for hell or shoot is for shit. And then there was the effect the word had on me. Unlike stupid, which washed over me, leaving me detached and deflated, snicker seared with pain. It would start in my chest and then course through my veins and flow throughout my entire body. I felt my blood would boil over with rage. That it might seep through my very pores and spill to the ground at my feet.

Never in my twenty-three years had I been called nigger. The word had been said in my presence, but no one had actually said it to my face. There were times I thought I heard the word in passing, muttered or said casually, but rather than check to see if I'd heard correctly, as I had done with Sophie, I'd pretend to ignore it, convinced I had heard wrong. I was astonished by the effect that a word, similar in sound, could have over me, as though it were the word itself.

"Don't call me that! Do you hear me? Don't you ever call me that again!" I'd snap at her. And then that sly grin would come. There was nothing more I could do except speak to Laura. I imagined what the conversation might look like. I ran it over in my head. Laura coming home, placing her shopping bags on the dining room table. "Hi, Melvie," she'd say brightly (although Sophie had abandoned this term of endearment, Laura would adopt it as her own). "How did everything go today?"

"Oh, fine, fine, the kids were great, except Sophie keeps calling me snicker, and every time she does it feels like she's calling me the *N* word, so yeah...."

It was absurd. The thought of an actual conversation with Laura brought me as much discomfort as the name calling itself. I thought I might vomit. How do I tell my boss, a white woman, that I think her three-year-old daughter is calling me the *N* word? It was outrageous. It was a slap in the face. It was insulting and accusatory. She must have gotten it from somewhere, perhaps Laura herself. Was that what I was implying? Was I calling Laura a racist? *Why on earth would you think such a thing?* She'd undoubtedly ask. *That's a horrible thing to say.* Suddenly the conversation would become less about what Sophie had called me and more about what I was implying about Sophie.

I felt like a wimp. I know now I was being hard on myself, but I didn't know it at the time. Instead of doing something about it, instead of taking matters into my own hands and taking action, I tried to pray the problem away. I prayed she might stop, that she'd forget all about the word the same way she had forgotten the word "stupid." There were times I thought my prayers had been answered. The day would be close to done, but before I'd go, she'd issue one final "snicker" before saying her good-byes, always out of earshot of Laura.

I turned on myself as well. I'd return home to the company of my critical voice and some name-calling of my own. It was like I'd picked up where Sophie had left off. Monday through Friday from nine to five, I was snicker. After work and on weekends, I was coward. It was like I was in a verbally abusive relationship with a three-year-old and myself. Like the two of us had joint custody.

The only thing that kept me sane during that time, oddly enough, was the possibility that it was all in my head. That I might be wrong. That the word did not mean what I thought it meant. Sophie loved to take words and redefine them as her own after all. She loved to invent her own words as well. Was snicker no different?

"Melva?"

"Yes, Ben."

"Sophie called me snicker."

I stopped what I was doing. Another shot of searing pain struck my chest. Was that the confirmation I had been looking for? Ben looked at me wearily, his face solemn and eyes wide. "She's just saying you're sweet like candy, Ben. Like a Snickers bar," I said, hoping it to be true. I watched him closely.

Ben looked at me almost pityingly. "No," he said seriously. "That's not what she's saying."

I had the feeling if I asked him directly what the word meant he would have told me, but I suddenly decided I didn't want to know. I was too afraid to know the truth. I couldn't handle it. And if the word meant what I thought it meant, I didn't want to put him in a position to explain it to me. Though I suppose I didn't want to put myself in a position to have to respond to it either. Besides, he looked at me as if I should know exactly what he was talking about, like it was a real word. I felt my chest might explode.

Though I have to admit there was some relief in Sophie

calling her brother snicker. To know that the word was not solely reserved for me, to know there was no racial connotation to it, at least not in her mind, was comforting. A snicker wasn't necessarily a black person but a person who annoyed her. Color didn't matter. And wasn't that Dr. King's dream after all? That every man, woman, and child be judged not by the color of their skin but by how much they annoyed you? I made Sophie apologize to Ben. I told her I never wanted to hear that word again. I told her it was a mean word that only mean people used, and since she was not that kind of person, she was not to use it. She looked at me with mild interest, and that sly grin splayed across her face.

"Sophie, do you understand me?" I repeated, raising my voice a little louder, and taking two steps to the right to turn off the TV.

"Yes," she said stubbornly, before turning away.

The next day Sophie called me snicker again.

"*I'm* telling you she's calling you nigger! Even the little boy is like, 'Yo, Melva, she's calling us nigger," Rob laughed, his thumb and forefinger moving at a rapid pace over the game control. "You're the only one who doesn't want to see it, or maybe you just don't want to do anything about it. Defense! Goddammit!"

Weeks passed and Sophie continued to use the word as if it were my name, and then one day she said it in front of Laura and I couldn't ignore it anymore. The opportunity had presented itself at last. I was on my way out the door. I said goodbye to both her and Ben, and then Sophie said straight to my face, "So long, snicker."

Ben's eyes seemed to pop out of his head. His mouth hung open in surprise. He threw a quick look to his mother and then slowly backed out of the room as if a bomb was about to go off. Laura's eyes flashed for a fraction of a second and then returned to their previous state, but her face stiffened as she spoke. "Thank you for everything, Melva. We'll see you tomorrow," she said hurriedly, in a voice much louder than necessary, as though she was trying to talk over Sophie, despite the damage having already been done.

"What did she just call me?" I asked Laura, looking straight at her. "She keeps calling me that. Do you know what that word means?"

"Oh, who knows." Laura waved her hand dismissively, unable to maintain eye contact. "Thanks again, Melva. See you tomorrow." Laura was practically shoving me out the door.

I don't know what went on behind the closed door of the Cooper household that night, but what I do know is that it was the last time Sophie Lindsay Carter Cooper ever called me nigger—oops, I mean snicker.

WELCOME TO VERMONT

South Hero, Vermont, is warm and welcoming. It boasts beautiful families and beautiful properties. The town has its own special brand of magic. I would not be surprised if it disappears after sundown or shows itself only to those who are in great need of it.

I fell under its spell the moment I arrived. Jessica, my old college roommate, and her mom had picked me up early that morning. Jess took the wheel first, and her mom let me sit up front, while she and their Golden Retriever, Lady, stretched out in the back. Nearly nine hours later we drove down a long road and pulled into the driveway of a small green cottage at dusk, and every day after seemed to top the day before.

I would not have thought it possible that my fondness for the place could rival Jessica's, but surely it had. Jessica carried a deep affection for her home state—to know her was to know her love for Vermont. The change in seasons brought about the most nostalgic feelings in her, but it was the summer season that seemed too wonderful for words. It deserved only a deep and plentiful sigh, a far-off look, and a curious grin—one which I now understood on a much deeper level.

I awoke each morning feeling rested and restored, full of purpose and possibility, ready to experience life and embark upon an adventure—like a real one, the kind you can't have in the city, the kind that involves nature and the elements. My time in Vermont was like the sayings on framed artwork and decorative pillows. *Dance like no one's watching. Love like it's never going to hurt. Live life to its fullest.*

Our entire stay culminated in the Clarence DeMar 5K/10K

Race held bright and early on the Fourth of July. Jessica had been training for weeks, but I had only just decided to run the race the day before. It seemed to be part of the Vermont experience and I didn't want to rob myself of it. I fell behind Jessica seconds after the race began, unable to keep up with her pace, but it didn't matter. Runners who passed me by, having turned around at the halfway mark and now making their way back to the finish line, cheered me on by name. Jessica seemed to know everyone in town, and by the end of my stay, it seemed everyone knew me even if introductions had never been made. They called out to me as I struggled to put one foot in front of the other. "There you go, Melva! Lookin' good, Melva! Keep it up, Melva! Yeah, Melva!" It was the middle school "mile run" all over again, only with words of encouragement and the overwhelming feeling of discovery of doing something new.

Later that evening, after a hot shower and a long nap, I stood in the grass at a backyard barbeque, enjoying the view of Lake Champlain beneath a massive starlit sky, eyeing my crush as he made his way down the long wooden staircase to the water bank, thinking how much I'd like to join him. The muscles in my legs were seizing up, still sore from the race I had run, but I didn't mind, I turned my gaze to the sky as fireworks soared in the air, lighting up the land below. The bursts and bangs, pops and sizzles were soothing, like listening to waves crash against rocks. It seemed remarkable to me that I might have missed this moment. Days before our departure my ex-boyfriend, Rob, now attending grad school in Maryland, returned to New York for a surprise visit. I had broken up with him a few months ago, the day after my twenty-fourth birthday. The breakup brought me closer to God. I think. I found it an act of divine intervention. I woke up that morning, saw him sitting on my couch watching TV, and knew we were over.

But after his most recent visit I entered into a deep depression. His surprise stay stirred up so many feelings of anxiety and anger, it was a wonder I didn't shut myself up in my apartment and close myself off to the world for weeks after he left. In some parallel universe the Melva that had turned down Jessica's invitation sat at home, listening to the now harsh sounds of fireworks from afar, watching *Independence Day* on TNT. I smiled sadly at that Melva, knowing she was content where she was because she could not know what she was missing out on, and also knowing that a part of her yearned for something more, a deeper experience, a palpable and powerful connection, one that did not stink of solitude.

I breathed in the cool night air and was filled with gratitude and a deep fondness for everyone around me. The fireworks ended and guests turned their attention away from the sky, carrying on with conversation.

"My son is obsessed with you," said the mother of a seven-year-old boy studying me closely. Sarah, Jessica's cousin, had had a few drinks. "Obsessed," she said again. "He loves your skin. I don't blame him. I'd kill for your skin tone."

Suddenly the South Hero spell was broken. Sarah's words shook me and woke me up from what seemed to have been a very deep sleep. It was like returning to work after a long weekend. Suddenly I was no longer Melva; instead, I was the black girl.

"I've been taking him to the mall lately just so he can see more black people," Sarah continued.

"Oh," I said. "That's...great."

On one hand, this mother seemed to be making a concerted effort to expose her son to people who didn't look like him, which I found...decent. On the other hand, I'm wondering is this for real? Do white people take their children on outings just to see black people? Like we're some exhibit at the science center or a new installation that just opened at the MET?

Sarah took another long swig of her drink. "You know," she continued, suddenly struck by a new talking point. "When I was young a very close friend of mine was a little black girl." *Here we go... Here we fucking go...* "I loved her. I wanted to be her," she said emphatically.

Jessica eyed her cousin nervously. I knew she was searching for a way out, a way to avoid the oncoming offense, the insensitive remark that was sure to come but was still one or two slurred words away. Jessica placed her hand on her cousin's arm. She might have given it a little squeeze, although I can't say for sure. It wouldn't have mattered though. Sarah was too inebriated to pick up on subtle social cues.

"One time we were in the bathroom together," Sarah recounted, "and she was in the stall next to mine and she reached her hand beneath my stall for some toilet paper and I screamed because I thought she was a monkey!" Sarah broke out into laughter. Jessica looked mortified.

"That's pretty awful," I said.

"I know!" she said, laughing gleefully. "Come to think of it...." *Please stop thinking.* "I don't think she was fully black. She definitely wasn't one hundred percent black. I think she was mulatto."

"That's offensive," I said abruptly. "That's definitely offensive."

"Is it?" Sarah asked.

"Yes," I said defiantly, before launching into a brief lecture on the term—its meaning, its roots, why it's derogatory. Sarah listened attentively and so did Jessica. I was disappointed to see that this was new information for her as well.

"What should I say then?" she asked. "Mixed?"

I grimaced. I don't really like the word "mixed" to describe a person's racial makeup. "I prefer bi-racial," I said.

A look of dawning and then, "I'm sorry," she said. "I'm not making you uncomfortable, am I?"

"No, not at all," I said honestly, and I was surprised at

just how true those words were. What had happened to my racially sensitive insecure self? Had it packed up and gone away? Was this part of the South Hero spell? Had it remained intact after all? A white woman, whom I had never met before, was rambling on about mulattoes and monkeys and yet my heart was still beating at its normal pace. I was offended, yes, but I wasn't wounded. Her words had hit me, but they had not hurt me. *What is this magic?*

Then, not wanting to give her the wrong idea, or think her words innocuous, I said, "But you *are* killing my buzz."

And she was.

Sarah looked slightly abashed. Jessica laughed nervously. "Come on, Mel," she said, grabbing my wrist, eyeing the empty drink in my hand. "Let's get you another." She motioned to my crush who had made his way back up the long wooden staircase and was now heading back inside the house. I grinned despite myself.

"I was so worried she was going to say something inappropriate," Jessica said, breathing a sigh of relief, as we made our way back inside the house, the distance between her cousin and I continuing to grow.

"She did," I said. "She definitely did."

We had overstayed our welcome—the hosts had already gone to bed. But I was determined to make my last night in South Hero count, to go out with a bang—literally. Connor, my crush, eased out of the chair we had been sharing and helped me up. We were trying to figure out where to go and what to do next when I said, "You can get me to do pretty much anything as long as you say, 'It's part of the Vermont experience.'"

Connor blushed but laughed appreciatively. "Good to know."

We said our goodbyes to the other remaining stragglers and stumbled out to the driveway. I looked up at the Vermont sky and was mesmerized by the stars. I fail to notice most of life's natural beauties—a bed of flowers, a sunset streaking the sky with red, yellow, and orange, or a ladybug crawling up a long blade of grass—but I will never overlook a starlit sky. "There's Polaris. The North Star," I exclaimed, too tipsy to stop myself. "North, south, east...yes, there's Orion in the west! Those three stars lined up in a row are his belt." Connor feigned interest but did it well. His brother Cameron motioned to Jessica and the two of them made their way to his car. Instinctively, I followed along. Connor grabbed my wrist and put his other hand on my waist.

"Oh no, you don't," he said, steering my drunken self to its new destination—the passenger seat of his car. "You're coming with me."

He opened the passenger side door and I collapsed inside. We arrived at his parents' house and made our way into the kitchen. It was dark and quiet inside. His family, who had attended the party as well, was already asleep. I scanned the kitchen and noticed a book tucked away by the napkin holder. "I love Zadie Smith," I gasped. Jessica and Cameron seemed to be caught off guard by my sudden outburst. Jessica shot me a look that seemed to say, *Shut up and look pretty!* But Connor was a gentleman. "Oh yeah? Our mom's reading it."

"She's one of my favorites," I said, having read her most recent book—the same one propped up on Connor's kitchen table—*White Teeth*. I saw it as a sign. I was doing the right thing. I was in the right place. Surrounded by the right people.

"Well, goodnight guys," Jessica said abruptly. "Bye, Mel." She leaned in, gave me a kiss on the cheek, squeezed my arm, then took Cameron by the hand and walked out of the kitchen. Connor and I were alone. I looked at him with what I'm sure was an expectant grin on my face, one that I hoped would say, *So now what?*

And he responded. "Want to go look at the stars?"

"I'd love to."

We went out to the deck. Connor lit candles to keep the mosquitoes away. We stared out at Lake Champlain and gazed at South Hero's starry sky. He pointed out Burlington to me and some other places I didn't care about, and then we were making out. Connor suggested we move inside and guaranteed the twin bed he'd slept in all his life was more comfortable than the wooden bench I was now straddling him on. He stood up with me still clinging to him.

"Wow. You're really strong," I said.

He shook his head. "You're really light," he said with a smile. God, he was cute. He gave me an extra heave and carried me back inside, down the steps to the basement, and into his bedroom.

The next morning was weird. Obviously. The spell seemed to have broken a little after sunrise when his mom walked in on us lying in his bed, carrying a laundry basket. Connor threw the covers over my head and pretended he was sleeping, and I slowly slid my feet back under the covers, so they could no longer be seen hanging over the edge of the bed. When his mom left with his dirty clothes, Connor looked upset.

"Do Jess and I need to leave through the window or something?" I asked.

"No, it's fine that you're here," he said sleepily. "It's just weird having my mom see me in bed with a girl." He sighed. "Well, we might as well get up now."

We got dressed and went upstairs and into the kitchen. We sat across from one another at the table, waiting for Cameron and Jessica to get up while his mom and sister bustled around the kitchen. Connor offered me a bowl of cereal. Everything they had was full of grains and oats and dried fruit. I thought of making a joke, asking if he had anything with sugar, food coloring, and artificial flavors in it but decided against it.

We sat in the living room after we ate. I would be flying

out later that day and was already beginning to feel nervous about what awaited me in New York—babysitting, auditioning, and being single for the first time in three and a half years. I picked up a magazine on the coffee table. One of the cover stories was the Duke rape case. I turned to the article, read a paragraph or two, and then put it back down quickly, thinking it might not be the best time to read up on the story of a young black woman who falsely accused a group of white men of raping her. And just like that it was back. My racial anxiety had returned.

"Should we see if Jessica and Cameron are up?" I asked.

"*You* can," said Connor. It was clear he was not going to interrupt his older brother in bed with a girl, the way his mom had done to him.

I was ready to get out of there. So I made my way back down the stairs and gently tapped on the door. "Jess," I whispered, but there was no response. *Please don't be having sex, please don't be having sex.* I cracked the door open and Jessica's head popped out from beneath the covers.

"Morning, Mel," she said in her high-pitched voice. Cameron was still asleep but was starting to come to.

"Hey, you wanna head out soon?" I asked.

"Give me one minute," she said.

Several minutes later we stood in the entryway saying our goodbyes. I was happy to see a smile return to Connor's face, and with it some semblance of the boy I'd slept with the night before. "Thanks for making me a part of your Vermont experience," he said with a grin.

Thank you for the warm welcome, a voice sang inside my head.

I kissed Connor on the cheek, squeezed his arm, walked out the door, and never saw him again.

Later that summer I sat on a blanket in Central Park with Jessica and her roommate, listening to the New York City Symphony, recounting our time in Vermont over wine and cheese—my first attempt at water skiing and running a race I hadn't trained for; hiking and biking; parties and picnics; a bonfire and backyard barbeque. Jessica's roommate listened to our adventures raptly, engrossed in our South Hero stories. A moment of silence passed between us. We sipped our wine, munched on our cheese, and listened to the musical score now swelling in sound, and then....

"I think you were, like, the only black person in a fifty-mile radius."

"Yeah, Jess," I said, looking up to the New York night sky, its stars slighted and unseen. "I think I might have noticed that."

SUMMER IN CENTRAL PARK

Two years out of college and Jess had remained one of my closest friends. Still, things did not feel the same in New York as they did in Vermont. The South Hero spell had officially broken and something between us had, too. I could feel each of us pulling away from the other. Something had shifted. It felt like she kept competing with me in a race I didn't know I had entered.

First, it was body image. I was sitting on my bed, changing my top, when she said, "It makes me so happy that your stomach hangs over your pants like that." After that, it was about work. She had started babysitting for the family I used to nanny for and found it necessary to remind me of it as often as she could. "I've completely replaced you at the Coopers," she'd say. "The kids love me." And then, it was boys.

We were on the lawn in Central Park with a spread of sandwiches and assorted snacks between us. Ethan, a guy I had been seeing, was coming to meet us. Unable to give him our exact location, I handed my phone over to Jess, but instead of giving him actual directions she told him to look for her in a short white sundress (something I could have done myself). Then she blushed and laughed, leaving me to wonder what he had said. A little while later, Ethan found us. I can't remember who he greeted first when he arrived, me or Jess, but I remember my ripped jeans and Juicy Couture purple terry cloth top went unnoticed while her sundress swished and swayed in the spotlight.

I couldn't stop thinking about how better suited they were for each other. And not because they were two well-dressed white kids with dirty blond hair who looked like they belonged on the cover of an Eddie Bauer catalogue or because of their shared love of skiing—a topic they went on and on about, as if purposefully trying to leave me out of the conversation—but because of the ease with which they interacted with each other, as if they had known each other for years. They talked and teased as if I wasn't there. As if they were the only two people in the park. Something about me and Ethan felt forced.

He didn't stay long. When he got up to say goodbye I half thought Jess might get up to go with him, but instead she returned to her spot on the grass, looking satisfied as she watched him walk away. I wondered if I'd see him again. I wondered if Jess was thinking the same.

"Want to hear something awful?" she asked.

Not really. She had just finished flirting with the guy I was sleeping with. I had no interest at all in anything she might have to say to me.

"Before Josh and I slept together..."—Josh was a white guy who had made me a card on my birthday the previous year. I liked him a lot and was rooting for him when it came to him and Jess but did not see it ending well for him—"... he was, like, should we use a condom? And I was, like, I don't know, should we? And he was, like, well probably...you have been with a lot of black guys."

Why was she telling me this?

"Isn't that awful?" she asked.

Only she looked like it wasn't awful at all but rather enjoyable, really, that someone other than her should recognize how many black guys she'd been with.

"Yeah," I said. "Pretty awful."

Jess was really into black guys. So was I. But I kept it to myself. She, on the other hand, talked of nothing else.

"I've dated more black guys than you have," she said. Jess

was never very good at keeping secrets and this was a big one. I had been waiting for her to say it for weeks. Still, I was not prepared when she finally did. Jess tried not to look too pleased with herself but was doing a poor job of it as a small smile flickered across her face. My heart did the usual plummet. It was a familiar feeling, her using me to feel better about herself, but she had never invoked race to do it. That was new.

Why are white people so bold when it comes to belittling my blackness? I expect to see it printed in the paper one day. Or spelled out in the sky.

Jess looked at me as though waiting for me to concede some long, hard-fought fight. I couldn't stand to see her looking so smug. And since the truth was of no use to me in that situation, I decided to go with a lie.

"No, you haven't," I said. "I dated black guys in high school."

I hadn't dated *anyone* in high school. Not really. My senior year I played mini golf with a black guy whose parents were friends of my parents, and once I went to the movies with an Indian guy I met through a mutual friend, but that had been it. I knew when I said it Jess didn't buy it. High school didn't count. She had been talking about black guys I had *slept* with. I knew that. She knew that. But it was the best I could do.

I didn't have a problem with Jess dating black guys. I had a problem with her boasting about it, throwing it in my face, turning it into a competition. I had a problem with her keeping score. I had a problem with her pulling rank, putting me in my place. I had a problem with her using black men as a measuring stick to tally her worth against mine. *I've dated more black guys than you have.* I'm more than you. More what, exactly? More black? More desired? More of what men—black men—want? I'm more. You're less.

It's a message I had heard over and over again and now I

was hearing it from a friend, someone I trusted, someone I cared about, someone whose family had welcomed me into their home, whose dad had tried to teach me how to water-ski, and whose mom had made me a chicken sandwich. I'm more. You're less. Whether it's intentional or not, it's a supremacist attitude. Her need to see me, not as an equal, but as someone she was superior to, and the disturbing thing is, she used race to do it.

A moment or two passed, and then Jess, determined not to drop the subject, continued. "You know, Laura asked me if you date black guys."

Laura was the woman I used to nanny for. The two of them had become very close. Close enough to discuss my sex life, apparently.

"Why would she ask you that?" I said, taken aback.

"Oh, I don't think she was judging you," said Jess. "I think she was just curious."

And so was I. I was curious as to *what the fuck* they thought my dating or not dating black men had to do with them. I was curious as to what they thought it might mean. I was curious as to why they were gossiping behind my back, like my blackness was the cover story of *Star* or *The National Enquirer*. I was curious as to what about me they'd really like to know. What were they getting at? *Do I date black guys?* Of course I date black guys. Without question. That was what upset me most about the discussion. That it *was* a question. And the fact that she had asked it left room for—no matter what Jess had said—judgment.

I had been introduced to Laura's curiosity before. She had asked me about the head scarf I was wearing when I spent the weekend babysitting at their second home in Connecticut. I had gotten out of bed to greet her after she returned home late one night. I stepped out of the guest bedroom and into the kitchen, saw her eyes roll to the top of my head, and then give a look like I was wearing a beer cap or something equally absurd.

"Is that for the hair?" she asked. *Uh, yes, Laura, this thing wrapped around my hair is for my hair. It's not holding my head together.* It was like she was getting this peek into black womanhood but didn't know what to do about it.

It was hard not to feel resentful. I resented Laura, Jess, and all the white people in my life who looked at me like I was a mirage, one which they had to constantly determine whether it was real or not. And I resented myself for not being able to do anything about it, not being able to say anything about it, not being able to stop it.

My resentment showed itself at a rooftop party Jess and her new roommate threw later that summer. The conversation had somehow turned to dating outside one's race; no doubt Jess had steered it that way. "Melva dates white guys," she offered up to the crowd.

"No, Jess," I said without thinking. "I don't date white guys. I fuck white guys."

Jess laughed, but everyone else went quiet. Her roommate was clearly bothered by what I had said. I got up and moved to a different part of the roof. I was in a strange mood all of a sudden. I had shocked myself by what I'd said. It had slipped out—the truth, that is. I wasn't dating white guys, not really, not at that point. And it's not because I didn't want to. I was hanging out with them, hooking up with them. Still, no one was actually pursuing a relationship with me. I didn't realize how much that upset me until that very moment.

After I stopped seeing a white guy I had met at a bar on Super Bowl Sunday, Jess made sure to tell me she'd run into him walking beside a woman who looked just like me. "Did she really look like me or was she just black?" I asked. "Uh, well, I didn't really see them up close," she admitted, caught off guard. I remember thinking this was her way of telling me that the guy I used to date was into black women. That he may have been interested in me only because I was black. That he, and maybe other guys I had been with, had a thing for black women. Of course, I don't know for sure if this was her intention. But it sure did feel like it.

In the end, Jess and I drifted apart and our friendship ended. A few years after we'd both moved to Los Angeles, I was invited to a birthday party of hers and arrived with my then boyfriend—a black guy. When she asked how the two of us met, I said online, and she burst into laughter (no one else did—they, in fact, looked a little embarrassed that she thought it was so funny), and I was reminded why we weren't close anymore.

We ran into one another again years later when I was on my way to a juice bar. "I'm married," was the first thing she said.

"I know," I said.

She then introduced me to her mother-in-law who was standing by her side. "How long have you lived in this neighborhood?" Jess asked me.

"Oh, I don't know," I said. "About four years." And we both laughed. I had forgotten we lived so close to one another.

"Can we be friends again?" she asked in her high-pitched voice.

"Of course," I said. But we didn't become friends again. In fact, we haven't spoken since.

HARRY AND THE HAMPTONS

There are two types of people who ride the Hampton Jitney: those traveling for work, and those traveling for pleasure. I was traveling for work. I had just been hired as a nanny for a family of four who split their time between their loft in Soho and their house in the Hamptons. I, on the other hand, was splitting my time between my bed and couch, rereading the Harry Potter books, waiting for the seventh and final installment to be released that summer.

Oh, that reminds me... I'm going to need time off.

I was scheduled to work the night of the Scholastic Bookstore's midnight release party, and because I was a live-in weekend nanny, I would not be able to attend, and thus would have to risk the final book being spoiled for me. I couldn't do it. I just. Couldn't. Do it. I had to go. It was a once-in-a-lifetime experience. Something to tell my grand-kids.

Nana, where were you the night the last Harry Potter book came out?

I was at the Scholastic Bookstore in New York City. They turned Mercer Street into Diagon Alley and there was a bright purple triple-decker Knight Bus parked outside the store. I waited in line for hours and hours to get the book at midnight, and then I raced home and read it with the rest of the world, warm in my bed.

Wowww....

Run along and play now.

In the months leading up to the release it seemed the entire city was reading, or rereading, the books. I felt like I was a part of an anonymous book club that met on park benches, on subway platforms, or in line at Starbucks. I'd spot New

Yorkers on street corners holding the book with one hand while hailing a cab with the other, or using it as a tray to carry a muffin or bagel back to their table, or tucked under their arm on a crowded train, a metro card stuck between the pages as a bookmark, and I'd wonder what chapter they were on. It was such an uplifting sight. Were Tinkerbell to sprinkle fairy dust on me, I could fly to Surrey and back. I've seen people get married, walk hand in hand with someone they love, nap with a newborn on their chest, play with a puppy, embrace a parent, hug a tree, and I'd think, *Oh, that's nice*, but show me someone reading a Harry Potter book and my heart fills with joy. I want to befriend each and every one of them. I want to run up to them and say—

Oh shit! Is this my stop? The doors to the Hampton Jitney closed and the bus began to pull away. *Time to leave Hogwarts, Melva! Close the book and get it together!*

"Sir!" I shouted to the driver. "Sir! Is this Southampton?"

Fucking shit. I'm going to miss my stop. I peered out the window. Although I had no idea what Southampton looked like, having never been before, I thought there'd be a sign welcoming me (or Hagrid to greet me—*okay, seriously, Melva, stop*). "Is this Southampton?" I repeated again, staring into the faces of strangers surrounding me, searching for confirmation.

The driver slammed the brakes and reopened the doors. I found my footing, shoved *Harry Potter and the Half-Blood Prince* into my bag, threw the bag over my shoulder, thanked the driver, and stumbled off the bus.

"There you are," said John, standing beside his convertible. "I was beginning to worry," he said, shaking my hand. He grabbed my bag, threw it into the car, and climbed into the driver's seat. "Thought you might have gotten lost."

I mumbled a soft-spoken "no," then climbed into the passenger seat next to him. *That. Was. Close.*

The Hampton Jitney continued along its path, and John and I sped off.

"First time on the Jitney?" John asked.

"Oh yes."

"How was the trip?"

"It was great!" *Much nicer than the Greyhound I'm used to.*
We drove down a pretty tree-lined street. The town reminded me of Sewickley. Weekenders strolled in and out
of shops. The scene looked like a photo from a magazine
called *Simply Suburban.* "So how long have you been coming
to Southampton?" I asked.

"Oh, not long, only about forty-four years," he said.
This guy. Fucking. Hilarious.

"So you must like it then," I said.

"It's grown on me."

"Has it changed much in forty-four years?" *Look at you,
Melva, and your savvy small-talk skills. Way to keep the conversation
moving and get this uncomfortable car ride done and over with.*

"Uh, here and there, I suppose," said John.

Way to drop the ball, John. Now what? Silence, as I searched
for something to say, then—*swish!* A jeep swerved in front of
John's convertible and then returned to its previous position.

"Out-of-towners," John said. "People come here from the
city for the weekend and don't know how to drive." I nodded
my head automatically, as if to say, *Out-of-towners. They're the
worst.* Silence again, then—*swish!* The jeep swerved in front
of John's convertible again. He stared at the jeep with an odd
expression on his face. "How much do you want to bet the
driver of that car is a woman?"

*Whoa. How much do you want to bet the driver of this car is an
asshole?* Without waiting for my reply, John switched lanes
then floored it. I held on to my hat, threatening to blow
off in the wind. John glanced to his right. The convertible
swerved a bit then drew level with the jeep. John glanced to
his right again.

"Ha! I knew it. I was right," he said triumphantly, glancing
at me as if congratulations were in order.

Wow, sexism so soon? I gave an obligatory nod. John, satisfied, continued to drive with a smear of smug splattered all over his face.

Soon we arrived at a large gate. John opened it and pulled into the driveway where two black SUVs were parked in front of a massive white house. Tall hedges wrapped around the perimeter of the property and shielded it from the street, sidewalk, and passersby. John grabbed my luggage and we made our way inside, the gravel crunching beneath our feet. A small child popped out from nowhere and greeted us at the door. It was six-year-old Ava. She wore a long nightgown and carried a stick in her right hand. "We're making stone soup, just like in the book."

"That sounds delicious," said John, sliding off his shoes in the entryway and walking into the kitchen to greet his wife, Annie, and their nine-year-old son, Christopher.

Annie was stirring a large pot on the stove. She, too, was in her pajamas, as was Christopher, who bounced a ball around the large kitchen table, chasing it as it rolled away from him and between the legs of the chairs. "We're seeing who can stay in their pajamas the longest," said Annie, with a nod to her children.

I wish I had known, I thought to myself. *I'm really good at that game.*

"Do you like Harry Potter?" Ava asked, eyeing me closely. A sudden rush of reassurance swelled inside me. "Do I!" I said, whipping out my copy of *Harry Potter and the Half-Blood Prince.* Ava bounced up and down on her tiptoes, waving her stick like a wand.

The next morning over breakfast Ava filled me in on who was who in their game of Harry Potter make-believe. "I'm Harry. And Mommy's Hermione. And Christopher is Ron."

"Who should Melva be?" asked Annie, placing a plate of chocolate chip pancakes in front of her daughter.

Ava took her time to think about it while picking her choc-olate chip pancakes apart with her fingers. "How about..." she said thoughtfully. "Angelina Johnson."

Annie caught my eye and winked, suppressing a knowing smile. I returned the smile but was not amused. Angelina Johnson was the only black-identified female character in the series. She was also one of the least interesting characters in the books. Ava might have asked me to play a potion bottle instead. I was reluctant to take on the role, but I tried to be a good sport about it and did it anyway. All I could think to say was, "Who wants to go outside for a game of Quidditch?" And then I started complaining about Madam Hooch. The kids ignored my feeble attempts and carried on with their game as usual. I couldn't win with Angelina. I asked to be Luna Lovegood instead. At least as Luna I could make them laugh. *Did you know dementors carry bunnies beneath their robes? Did you know the Crumple-Horned Snorkack squirts pumpkin juice out of its nose when it sneezes? Did you know the Minister for Magic is really a muggle named Murray?* I could go on.

After breakfast the game moved outside to the backyard. Annie and John stood on the patio deep in discussion while the kids and I played by the pool. And then Christopher and Ava got into an argument, which escalated quickly. Voices were raised, Ava was close to tears, and Christopher was teetering on a tantrum. John and Annie showed no signs of interfering: my first test. During my interview John had asked me about my method of discipline. Having never considered it before, I told him I take on whatever method the parents use, taking away privileges, time outs, that sort of thing. He told me that he and Annie always use distraction to pull the kids' attention away from whatever it is that's upsetting them. And that's what I did.

I ran over to Christopher and pretended he was reenact-ing the werewolf transformation scene in *Harry Potter and the*

Prisoner of Azkaban. I took on the role of Sirius. Grabbing hold of him I bent down to his level. "Remus my old friend, have you taken your potion tonight? You know the man you truly are, Remus. This heart is where you truly live. This heart here. This flesh. This only flesh."[4] Christopher and Ava, recognizing the lines, began to laugh. I turned to Ava and told her to run, and then turned my attention back to Christopher. *"Remus! Remus!"* I let go of Christopher. He chased after Ava. I let out a howl like Hermione does in the movie, making Christopher change directions and run after me instead. And the game of Harry Potter werewolf tag ensued. And from that moment on the game changed. I was no longer cast as Angelina but as Sirius instead. Christopher was Remus instead of Ron. Annie became James instead of Hermione. And Ava was Lily instead of Harry. And every weekend our game of pretend picked up from where it had left off the weekend before.

"Hello, Black!" said Ava when I entered the playroom with bowls of fruit and bottles of water. Ava had taken to calling me by my character's surname in our ongoing game of Harry Potter make-believe. And as Sirius's last name was Black, I was known as, well, Black. At any given moment she'd turn to me and say:
"There you are, Black."
"Where've you been, Black?"
"How's it going, Black?"
"Can I have a snack, Black?"
"What do you want to do next, Black?"
Black, Black, Black, Black, Black.
But all I heard was:
"I can't believe you're black."

---

[4] Kloves, Steve, and Gary Oldman. *Harry Potter and the Prisoner of Azkaban.* Amazon Prime video streaming service. Directed by Alfonso Curaón. Burbank, California: Warner Bros. Pictures, 2004.

"Did you know you're black?"

"How come you're black?"

"Have you always been black?"

And finally, "You're black."

I tried to ignore it but couldn't. She'd say it over and over again. I felt that she, like so many others, wanted to remind me that I was black, in case I had somehow forgotten. And I hated that. I wanted it to be nothing, no big deal—but it was, to me, anyway. Years of being singled out, silenced, and shamed for being black was showing itself in how I responded to a little girl who was only playing pretend. Or was she? I couldn't help but think there was more to it than that. That there was a deeper question being asked. Something unsaid that needed to be said. Was this her way of bringing up race? Was there something she didn't understand that she needed made clear? Was there something she needed to talk about? I had to do something. It was only a matter of time before she'd start calling me Black in public. And then what?

"Hey, Evans," I said. Thinking it best to handle this while in character, I addressed her by her character's surname too. "Why don't you call me by my nickname Padfoot instead of Black?"

"Why don't you want to be called Black?" she asked.

Again, I decided it was best to stay in character. "You know how much I dislike my family, Evans. They're a bunch of slimy, pureblood, muggle-hating Slytherins. I don't want anything to do with the Black family name. I'd change it if I could."

Ava looked satisfied by my response and started calling me Padfoot instead. Only her commitment to character could make her remember to do such a thing. Relieved, I thought the matter had been resolved until I walked into the playroom one day, again with bowls of fruit and bottles of water and heard Annie say, "Why don't we ask Melva what she thinks?" Annie was sitting on the floor alongside Ava. "Melva," she went on to say, "Ava was wondering if Bellatrix, Narcissa, and Andromeda would have been referred to as the Black girls when they were younger since their last name is Black. What do you think?"

Clearly, Annie wanted to run this by me first before I heard Ava mentioning "those Black girls" in passing. I wondered if she was expecting me to give her daughter the talk about race she herself could not find the words for? To tell Ava that, although Bellatrix, Narcissa, and Andromeda's last name was Black, referring to them as "the Black girls" would mean something different. It sounds like you're referring to their race or the color of their skin. Because people with dark skin, brown skin, like me, are called "black." How easy the words come to me now. "Uh, maybe they could be called the Black sisters instead..." I offered up meekly. Not that it made much of a difference—or any sense to a six-year-old. Surely, Ava was wondering why it was okay to say "the Black sisters" but not "the Black girls." But if she was, she didn't ask. Annie nodded her head like the matter had been resolved. And I went back to playing pretend, a little disappointed in myself.

During the months I worked for the Parkers, Ava grew very attached to me. It seemed I hadn't been hired as her nanny but as her permanent playmate. Every Friday night I'd arrive at the Parkers' loft in Soho, and Ava would grab me by the hand and greet me like an old friend she had just reunited with on the Hogwarts Express. The game was nonstop. When she refused to go to the bathroom before leaving the house, I'd get her to go by pretending we were visiting the bathroom Moaning Myrtle lived in to make Polyjuice Potion. When I needed her to show me which clothes to pack for the weekend, or how to work the TV, I'd remind her that it was her duty to help me. After all, she was a prefect, and I only a "first year." When she didn't want to brush her teeth before bed, I'd point her toothbrush at her mouth, wave it like a wand, and shout, "Alohomora!"

It was hard to tell who was enjoying herself more—Ava or me. In many ways it was a dream job. As if the Universe had brought Annie, Ava, Christopher, and me together to enjoy the final few moments before the last Harry Potter book came out. When we weren't playing Harry Potter, we were watching Harry Potter. When we weren't watching Harry Potter, we were listening to Harry Potter. When we weren't listening to Harry Potter, we were discussing Harry Potter.

"What color skin do you think Dean Thomas has in the books?" asked Ava.

"Uh," I began, a little thrown off, "he has the same color skin I have."

"In the movies, yes, but in the books, no," Ava told me.

We were having dinner. Annie, overhearing the conversation, tore her attention away from Christopher, and began to speak in a slightly higher register. "It's interesting, isn't it? When you read the books you imagine the characters to look one way and then you see the movie and they look another way," she said simply.

"No, it's written in the books as well," I said. "When Dean's first introduced in *Harry Potter and the Sorcerer's Stone* he's described as having brown skin."

Annie went quiet.

Ava said, "Are you sure?"

Look, kid, don't try to tell me who the black characters in Harry Potter are. "Positive," I said.

Ava looked at Annie. Annie looked at Ava. I went back to eating my food. That night, before bed, I'm almost certain Ava asked Annie to check to see if I was right. I was, of course, but not entirely. The book says Dean is black.

It does not say he has brown skin. Had I been right, had Dean been described as having brown skin, instead of being black, I think Ava might have registered and retained that information a bit more. After all, she knew what having brown skin meant. I don't think she knew what being black meant. When she suggested I play Angelina Johnson in our first game of pretend I don't think it was because she (or Annie, really) had read in the books that Angelina was black. It was because she had seen in the movies that Angelina was brown. Brown is a color. Black is a race. Ava knew nothing about race. Annie, of course, did. Why didn't she know Dean was black? Perhaps it was because she didn't *need* to know Dean was black? It wasn't impactful to her like it was to me. Part of privilege is overlooking that which doesn't affect you. Perhaps Annie was so used to seeing herself in the stories she read she was unable to see anyone else. I don't know. But if Annie overlooks race in a children's book, where else in the world, in her life, does she do the same? She had read the books and listened to the books on CD almost as much as I had. Still, she didn't know Dean was black. Meanwhile, her son, Christopher, didn't know *I* was black.

"Are you African American?" Christopher asked as I was tucking him into bed one night.

"Yes," I said. "Yes, I am."

"Thought so," he said.

"Why do you ask that, Christopher?"

"Oh, you wouldn't understand," he answered back.

And on that curious note he turned over and went to sleep. I stood there stumped. Why wouldn't I understand? Because I'm black? Because I'm African American? Was this a dig? Or something kids say when they don't want to talk anymore? It seemed Christopher had just learned the word African American and was trying it out for the first time, leaving me to wonder the nature of the conversation in which he had heard it.

Ava, on the other hand, was still curious about color. When I told her I had played Helena in Shakespeare's *A Midsummer Night's Dream*, after she and Annie had read a kids' edition of the play, she asked, "Did you have to dye your skin white?" *Did I have to dye my skin white?*

It was as if I had been hit by a Bludger (see Harry Potter books one through seven).

Ava was one of the brightest kids I had ever met. A Ravenclaw for sure. She was also one of the most imaginative kids I had ever met. She believed herself to be a witch and was convinced that she, like Harry, would receive a letter from Hogwarts in five years' time. And yet, she couldn't imagine me as Shakespeare's Helena, not without a dye that would somehow turn my skin white. If, in her imagination, the color of my skin had its limitations, what then did that say about her reality?

I took a deep breath while she waited to hear what I had to say. "You know how sometimes you pretend to be Harry when we play Harry Potter, even though Harry is a boy and you're a girl," I said to her. "It's like that. When you make believe you can be whoever you want to be." Ava looked at me like she was still trying to work something out.

One afternoon, I was making my way upstairs from the basement with orders of fruit and bottles of water. John and Annie had invited over their friends David and Deborah and their two kids. When I walked into the kitchen I heard Deborah, a petite, chatty woman who looked like she lived on the tennis court, say, "I mean, really remarkable, this man. Think of everything he's been through. Everything he's had to overcome. African American. Gay. Born and raised in the South. Unbelievable."

I didn't know who Deborah was talking about but it didn't matter. I opened the fridge, feeling flushed. I knew I was hearing something I wasn't supposed to hear.

"I don't doubt that the man is remarkable," John chimed in. "I just don't think it has anything to do with the fact that he's a gay black man from the South."

Annie and David remained quiet, unwilling to take sides in the John and Deborah matchup. I finished preparing a tray for the kids, then carried it back downstairs. I took a seat on the wrestling mat that covered the basement floor, my back against the wall, taking a breather while the kids played and ate their snacks. What John said hadn't surprised me. John was a straight, wealthy white man from New York. He can't see what makes a gay black man from the South remarkable because, by contrast, it would make him *un*remarkable. It's the struggle. It's overcoming that struggle, surviving that struggle. That's what makes people from marginalized communities remarkable. John can't see that, though. He has to protect his privilege.

John's parents had a house in the Hamptons, too. One weekend they hosted a pool party for their kids, grandkids, and friends. Annie made it a point to introduce me to a black woman who was at the party but to no one else. I was watching the kids play in the pool when I heard John's mother say to Annie, "Doesn't she swim?" I had only stuck my feet in the water. "Of course she does," I heard Annie say. "She just forgot her bathing suit this weekend."

Later, I was making my way through the grounds—it wasn't a yard—when Hailey, Christopher, and Ava's four-year-old cousin, cornered me and said, "You ripped it!" I had no idea what she was talking about. I bent down to her level to better understand her. "You ripped it," she repeated, this time motioning with her hands like she was tearing a piece of paper. Ripped what? "You ripped off your white skin!" Oh. "No, sweetheart," I said with a sigh. "I didn't."

The voices buzzing above us tried to drown her out. They intensified, as though to mask her tiny voice. I stole a glance at those around us—her parents were only a short distance away—family friends, cousins, aunts, and uncles, all stood within earshot.

"You did! You ripped off your white skin. Now you have brown skin." I continued to shake my head. Hailey wouldn't hear of it. It was like she was scolding me, like she wanted to know why I would do such a thing. Or wanted to find out how it might have happened, so she might prevent such a thing from happening to her. In her mind, my white skin had been ripped off and the brown skin I had was all that remained. Strangely, I didn't take offense. I knew it wasn't her fault.

"No, sweetheart," I said again, shaking my head. "I did not rip off my white skin," I said with a forced calm. "I never had white skin." It was like I was revealing the big twist in an M. Night Shyamalan movie. "This is my skin. This is the skin I was born with. Brown skin." Each word cost me something I'm still unable to identify. I waited for a response. She picked up her basket full of fruit and veggies from the garden and drifted off. I returned to the edge of the pool, dipped my feet back into the water, and took in my surroundings.

Why don't these kids know about black people?

Why is it my job to teach them?

As time passed, it became clear that race was an ongoing conversation in the Parker household, and although the specifics were unclear, I was getting some pretty big clues. One afternoon, Christopher, Ava, Annie, and I were sitting at the kitchen table having lunch when Christopher brought up something peculiar. He had a large book open on the table and was eager to share the discoveries he had made.

"When someone kills himself it's called suicide," he said. "When someone kills someone else it's called homicide. The root word means man."

Annie and I listened with feigned interest, or at least I did. Ava had checked out completely and was silently eating her food.

"The killing of a sibling is fratricide." I was nodding my head at all the right places, wondering why we were talking about that, and when could we get this boy some new reading material. Murder doesn't really make for suitable family meal conversation. "The killing of a parent is matricide or patricide," Christopher continued and then, struck by a new thought, said, "Hey, the killing of black people—"

"Christopher!" Annie cut in.

"Would be called *negrocide!*"

Uh, did that boy just invent a word for the killing of black people?

"What did you say, Christopher?" I asked, although I had heard him perfectly.

"The killing of black people would be called negrocide," he repeated.

"Well, no, not necessarily, Christopher," Annie rushed in. "The killing of the Jews during the Holocaust was called genocide."

Christopher considered that a moment before asking to be excused. The kids left the kitchen and returned to the playroom, leaving Annie and me alone to clear the table.

"I hope what Christopher said didn't offend you," she said.

"Oh no, of course not," I lied.

"I mean, you could see the point he was trying to make, right?"

"Right. Yeah. Of course."

Annie was only making matters worse, putting me in a position to have to agree with her, to excuse what her son had said. How did we get here? A few weeks ago Christopher hadn't known the word African American, and now, suddenly, he knew the word Negro. Who taught him the word Negro?

I didn't know how often race came up before I started

working as Christopher and Ava's nanny but it certainly was coming up a lot after.

On movie night Ava and I sat on the couch with a bowl of popcorn. The last preview to come on before the start of the movie was a film that took place during the Civil Rights era. We watched the preview in complete silence. I glanced over at her as one disturbing image after another flashed before us. She stared intently at the screen, a hard expression on her face. I could almost see the wheels turning inside her mind. I could almost hear the clicks as things slid into place. When it was over, her expression softened. And I knew that in that three-minute preview, she understood something she had never understood before.

Then one night, back in the city, I was giving Ava a bath. We had put our game of pretend on pause, but when Ava spoke it was in Hermione Granger's bossy British accent. "In school we've been studying the Underground Railroad," she said. *Oh no.* "The runaway slaves used to sing songs on their journey north. Do you know this one?"

Ava began to sing a deep mournful song I'd never heard before. The song went on for longer than I expected, and I had to suppress an urge to laugh. "No, I don't know that song, Ava," I said when she had finished.

"It's an old African American folk song," she said indignantly. "I would have thought that *you* of all people would know *that*."

Hold up. Now a six-year-old is shaming me for not knowing an African American folk song, when weeks ago, she and her brother hadn't known what African American was. White privilege starts early.

"You know, Ava," I began heavily. "Just because I'm African American doesn't mean—"

"Oh, I know, I know!" she cut me off. Clearly she'd had this conversation before. A few moments passed between us, and then she said, "Well, do you at least know 'Follow the Drinking Gourd'?"

"Yes," I said, losing my patience, "I know 'Follow the Drinking Gourd.'" Ava looked satisfied at this and then dunked her head under the water.

When it came time to ask for the weekend off to read the new Harry Potter book, I went to Annie, not John. "I understand, of course," she said, "but John will have a problem with it." *Yeah, I thought he might.* "I'll talk to him," she said.

The conversation hadn't gone well. I could tell by the way John treated me after. He wouldn't speak to me and kept a stony expression on his face. But I didn't care. I got what I wanted. In the hours before the book came out, I put the final touches on my Harry Potter presents for the kids, a small package with a humorous Harry Potter T-shirt inside. I addressed the package to their precise location and loaded it with stickers that said Owl Post. They were happy to have it, but it was Annie who seemed the most taken by the gifts. I met the three of them Friday night outside the back entrance to the Scholastic Bookstore where the street had been transformed into Diagon Alley. The kids had wanted to go to the Scholastic release party as well, and I had agreed to help out.

After a couple of hours Annie left with the kids, and I stayed behind to rejoin the line and pick up the book with a couple of friends. When I got my book at midnight, I got theirs too, along with the audiobook they'd ordered on CD. Afterwards, I went to their building to drop off their book and CD set with the doorman, and then I returned to my apartment to read. I finished the book forty-eight hours later.

I read *Harry Potter and the Deathly Hallows* at least two more times that summer before deciding to move to Los Angeles. As an actress, I felt I had exhausted every opportunity there was for me in New York. It was time for a change. When

I told Annie, her first concern was for Ava and how hard she'd take it. I told her I'd come back to visit. "That's what everyone says," she said sadly. But I stuck to my word. At least in the beginning. For the first couple of years after my move, I would drop by to see them when back in the city visiting friends. On one of my return trips, Annie told me that they never really played make-believe anymore. It wasn't the same after I left. It was hard to hear. During my last weekend at work, Christopher, Ava, Annie, and I played the most epic game of Harry Potter make-believe yet. We stayed in character the entire weekend. It was a lot—even for me. On my last night Annie said she didn't want me to leave until Ava was asleep, so I read to her until she drifted off. And then I was gone.

Amanda, Christopher, and Ava's weekday nanny, was a white South African woman who grew up during apartheid. She was tall and attractive with long blonde hair. She could have been a veela—or a descendant of one (see *Harry Potter and the Goblet of Fire*). She was always impeccably dressed and was never seen without her Louis Vuitton handbag hanging from her arm, a gift from one of the families she had worked for. She spoke in a thick South African accent, which gave the impression of someone poised and polished.

We became friends one weekend when John and Annie asked us to drive the kids up to Southampton together. The following day we took the kids into town and I got a funny feeling while walking alongside her. "Now everyone thinks you're the mom," I said. "But I'm still the nanny." She smiled sadly.

Before my move to Los Angeles we sat on the couch in my studio apartment drinking wine and eating takeout. I asked her about growing up in South Africa and the impact of apartheid on her.

"I thought black people were dirty and dumb," she

admitted. "I'm not proud of it. It's what I was taught. And I'm really ashamed."

"How did you change your thinking?" I asked.

"I left home. I came to the U.S. I went to school and I got educated."

"What other things were you taught?" I asked. I was suddenly struck by our friendship.

"All sorts of terrible things," she said uncomfortably. "That black people carried disease. That light-skinned blacks were better than dark-skinned blacks. Now I know better," she said.

"Then why don't you date outside your race?" I asked. Amanda had started online dating and told me the settings on her profile. Seeking white men who made $100,000 a year or more.

"I just don't think I'd have anything in common with someone outside my race."

"You and I have stuff in common," I reminded her.

"I mean, different cultures," she said.

"Yeah, but you might have more in common with someone who's Asian American than some white guy who grew up in France."

"I don't know, Melva," she said, clearly wanting to change the subject. "I just don't want to date outside my race."

A moment passed between us. "Do you still want to be my friend?" she asked.

"Of course," I answered back. "Don't be silly."[5]

We sat in silence in my studio apartment, unsure of where to take the conversation next.

---

5 Amanda and I stayed friends for a few years after my move to Los Angeles. Then our friendship would exist only on Facebook until, that is, I decided to hide her anti-Obama posts from my feed. After the 2016 election, I put up an anti-Trump post and she commented on it, saying how he was going to be a great president for all of us. I clapped back. Telling her that pro-Trump propaganda belonged on her page, not mine.

"The Parkers really liked you, Melva," she said after a while. "They thought you were smart."

I never told Amanda all of the racially tinged remarks that were said when I was working for John and Annie, but I did share with her one story that still bothered me. One weekend John and Annie were going to a party and they were going to take the kids with them, so they wanted me to come along, too. Annie told me about it in advance, so I made sure to bring something nice to wear. At the last minute they decided not to bring me, but it was really awkward the way it was done. Minutes before they left, Annie asked John if he thought they needed me to come. John said, "I don't know. What do you think?"

Annie said, "I don't know. What do you think?" They went back and forth like that a couple more times before deciding not to take me.

"If it had been you," I said to Amanda. "They would have taken you." Amanda considered this. "And there was this costume party they went to once in the city," I continued. "Annie told me the hosts were famous for their costume parties, but that they could be really distasteful. She told me that one year they hired black men—only black men—to carry the hostess into the party. I just wondered if there was more to it than that...."

Amanda knew what I was getting at. She sat in silence for a while, perhaps knowing more than she was letting on, and then said, "I don't know, Melva. I really don't think the Parkers are racist."

"Yeah," I said. "Neither do I."

TIMOTHY AND THE TERRIBLE, HORRIBLE, NO GOOD, VERY BAD DAY

As a nanny I've been apologized to hundreds of times, but no apology was worse than six-year-old Timothy's. Not because he didn't mean it, but because he did. He looked dejected. Defeated. Like he was apologizing for the death of his favorite superhero, which he had somehow caused. What's worse is that I knew he would remember that apology for the rest of his life. He had been shamed for what he had said. And we always remember shame. I know I do.

Bill had barely walked through the front door when Matt, his ten-year-old son, pulled him aside. "Dad, can I talk to you?" he said.

"Yeah, sure, bud. What's up?" said Bill, recognizing the note of seriousness in his eldest son's voice. Matt motioned to the entryway and Bill followed him out of the kitchen and down the hall where they wouldn't be overheard. A sudden foreboding came over me. I knew what the talk was about. It was about me. And Timothy. And what he had said to me in the car that day. And the last thing I wanted was for Bill to get involved. Bill was as surly and temperamental as his six-year-old son. Why couldn't Carol have come home first?

I stood in the kitchen, searching for something to do. My eyes landed on the sink full of dishes. Bill and Matt took their time talking. I couldn't hear the conversation that was happening between them, but I didn't need to. Matt seemed just as disturbed by what Timothy had said to me as I was. Moments passed, and then....

"Melva!" Bill's booming voice carried into the kitchen. He stormed in and met me at the sink, his shoulders hunched over and one hand resting on the counter. Out of the corner of my eye I saw Matt sneak out of sight. "What did Timothy say to you in the car today?" Bill demanded.

It suddenly became clear that Matt did not tell his father exactly what Timothy had said, only that it was really bad. Perhaps he had found it too awful to repeat. I didn't know if I could repeat it myself. And I suddenly resented that Matt made me do so. And then, for one strange moment, I actually felt sorry for Bill. He had no idea what he was walking into or the bomb I was about to drop on him.

We had been in my car and running late. I hadn't known how to get where we were going, and Timothy was pissed. I had upset him. I had told him he couldn't bring the corndog he was eating into my car. I had made him wrap it up and put it in the refrigerator to save for later. I had enforced a new rule and I was sticking to it—no eating in Melva's car, only water was allowed. Bill and Carol had graciously backed me up on this, saying, "Melva's car, Melva's rules."

It must have been a really good corndog because Timothy put up such a fight for it. "Why can't we take the minivan?" he demanded.

"Because the minivan doesn't have navigation and I don't know where I'm going." I was still new to Los Angeles and couldn't drive outside the neighborhood I lived in or worked in without using navigation.

Timothy let out a roar of frustration. And when he spoke his tone was harsh and hateful. "I'm having a terrible, horrible, no good, very bad day because of the *brown girl* in the front seat!"

My foot hit the brake. I put the car in park. There had been a collision, and yet there was no evidence of one at all. No bruises, no scratches, no cuts to speak of and yet I knew I was hurt.

"Timothy!" Matt bellowed from the backseat. "That is not okay!" he said fiercely. He unbuckled his seat belt and leaned forward into the front seat to speak to me, and when he did his tone was soft and sweet. "Melva..." he said tentatively, "Are—are you okay?"

I almost said yes. I almost said, "Yeah, Matt, I'm fine, thanks for asking." I was moved by his response, both touched and taken aback by his reprimanding his brother and his reaching out to me. I appreciated it. I did. I didn't know many ten year olds who would have responded the way Matt had. He'd done everything right. It made me feel hopeful. Proud. But the truth was I wasn't fine. I felt like shit. God, I felt like shit. And saying otherwise would have only let Timothy off the hook. And that I couldn't do.

"No, Matt, I'm not okay," I said. "I'm not okay at all with what Timothy said." Matt sat back in his seat and buckled himself back up again. I uttered a few feeble words to Timothy, regained my composure, and drove off.

Bill was speechless, as I knew he would be.

"I...I don't..." he stammered. "I, uh, don't even think he knows what he's saying," Bill spluttered.

Oh, I think he knew exactly what he was saying. I think he was trying to use the color of my skin against me, to hurt me, and he did.

"I've never heard him say anything like that before," said Bill. *Well, that might be because you spend most of your time in Santa Monica, Bill,* I wanted to say. *Try taking him downtown and see what comes out of his mouth then.* "What did you say to him?" Bill asked.

Oh, that was clever, I thought. Let's first concern ourselves with how I handled the situation since you seem to be at a loss as to how to handle it yourself. I told him *I* was having a terrible, horrible, no good, very bad day because of the little white boy in the back seat—what do you think I said to him, Bill?

"I told him that wasn't nice," I said lamely. "I told him he has to be careful of the things he says because words can hurt."

Bill nodded his head in approval, and then bellowed, "Timothy!" Timothy was in the family room but I could see him from the kitchen. His head poked out from behind the couch. Bill stormed in and turned off the TV, then bent down to face his youngest son. I caught a glimpse of Matt peeking his head into the kitchen and then pulling it out again. "Timothy, what did you call Melva in the car today?" Timothy shrugged his shoulders, his head bent down, looking sullen. "Did you call her the brown girl?"

I wanted to die. Please somebody kill me right now. A middle-aged white man was talking to his six-year-old son about the color of my skin in the room next to me. Please somebody make it stop.

Timothy nodded his head.

"Why would you call her that?"

Timothy looked around, searching the room for a reason, and then said, "I forgot her name." Bill gave him a that's-bullshit look. I saw Matt poking his head out from the hallway again, straining his ears to hear.

"We don't refer to people by the color of their skin. It isn't nice. Do you understand me?" Timothy nodded his head. "We don't refer to people by the way they look, period. If they're big or small, tall or short, fat or thin, it doesn't matter what people look like. We call them by their names. Do you understand me?"

"Yes." Timothy seemed to understand the severity of the situation. He spoke in a low voice and looked utterly ashamed of himself.

"Now go and apologize to Melva."

Timothy walked over to me. "Melva," he said painfully. He looked like he was sitting in a doctor's office waiting to get a shot. "I'm sorry."

"That's okay," I said a little too quickly, wanting to put him, both of us really, out of our misery. "Don't worry about it."

"Timothy!" Bill said sternly. "Come here." Timothy walked

back over to Bill who continued to kneel on the floor. "Was that a good apology? Or a bad apology?"

Oh Christ, Bill! Put that puppy down already. Can't you see it's in pain? Can't you see it's suffering? I couldn't stand to be there a minute longer. I felt like I was at somebody's wake, staring at a dead body in an open casket, witnessing death or something like it. I wanted to run out the door. Oh, what would I have given to be stuck on the 405 right then? It seemed to take Timothy three whole minutes to walk from his dad back to me. His head was so low all I saw was a mane of messy brown hair. When he looked up at me his face was splotchy and there were tears in his eyes.

"Melva," he said again, his voice wobbly and strained.

"Yeah, Timothy," I said, helping him along.

"I'm r-r-really s-s-sorry I called you the b-b-brown girl in the c-c-car today."

"Thank you, Timothy. Thank you for your apology. I really appreciate that."

Timothy turned back to his dad to see if he approved. Bill nodded his head, then escorted his son out of the kitchen and up the stairs to get ready for bed.

"I'll see you tomorrow, Timothy!" I hollered up at him.

"B-bye," he said sadly.

I finished the last of the dishes, grabbed my jacket and bag, and then turned around to find Matt facing me with an embarrassed look on his face. "He's just a kid, you know."

"Yeah, Matt, I know."

"I mean…he's only six. He doesn't even know who Martin Luther King is."

I smiled despite myself. Matt gave a half-smile back.

And with that, I said goodbye and walked out the door.

MATCHMAKER

I knew I loved Libby when she did for me what no other white person in my life would—she set me up with a black guy. My friend Amy had tried to do the same with her brother's roommate, a dentist who lived 3,000 miles away from me in New York. But when she mentioned the idea to her brother before my upcoming trip to the East Coast he shied away from it, saying it would be racist if the only reason she'd be setting us up was because we were both black. Great, I thought, as Amy relayed that to me over the phone, now I have to stay single because your brother is afraid of being racist. Really great. Libby, on the other hand, was not afraid of being racist because Libby was twelve. Marcus was her seventh-grade ethics teacher, and I was her best friend's nanny.

I knew Marcus was black the moment Libby mentioned him to me. I didn't need to see his picture posted on her school's website to know for sure. I already did. It was the only real reason Libby and her friends thought we would be so cute together and wanted to set us up to begin with. But did I mind? Not a damn bit.

"You know, if the two of you get married you'll have to make her your maid of honor," Libby's mom, Joan, said to me in passing. I let out a laugh but Joan did not. Joan was serious. Her face was stoic and still. She looked like she wanted me to give her my word right then and there that her daughter would be included in my wedding party, but I wasn't prepared to make that kind of commitment. Maid of honor is a lot of responsibility for a twelve-year-old. She was a bridesmaid at best.

Marcus and I hadn't had our first date yet but it was a comfort to know that I wasn't the only one thinking that far ahead. If Marcus and I *did* get married, if he was, in fact, *the one*, the father of my unborn children, then that would validate my nanny career. Wouldn't it? When people ask me how I met my husband I could say, "While working as a nanny," and it would all be worth it.

"I never dated a black man," Joan went on to say.

Wait, what? Why are you telling me this?

"Oh," I said in response. What was I supposed to say? Oh, that's too bad? I'm sorry to hear that? Joan kept looking at me like it was still my turn to talk. To her, it was the start of a new conversation, but to me, it was the end. The last thing I wanted to do was talk to a married middle-aged white woman about why she had never dated a black guy.

Today, I might entertain the idea and be a bit more curious, as I felt she, in that moment, might be betraying an unconscious bias, which I would have wanted to know more about. But back then, the conversation made me uncomfortable, and I had no idea how to deal with that discomfort. I think, too, some part of me realized Joan's statement wasn't really about Joan. It was about me. Joan didn't want to discuss the type of men *she* had or hadn't dated. She wanted to discuss the type of men *I* had or hadn't dated. I knew her well enough to know that her way of *getting* information was *giving* information. For instance, she once told me, again in passing, how much she weighed. "I can't gain a pound over 130," she said to me in confidence.

"Oh," I said.

Again, Joan looked at me as if she was hoping for me to say something more. I had noticed her eyeballing me up and down as if trying to guess my weight. We were about the same height and looked to be about the same size, but that wasn't good enough for her. She wanted to know the number on the scale. Therefore, she thought she'd share her weight with me, hoping that I would then share my weight with her. Give information, get information. That was her strategy. But it didn't work on me. I didn't reveal my weight. And I didn't tell her anything about the men I had or hadn't dated. Instead I made my excuses and continued on my way.

I think Joan needed to find a way to say what wasn't being said. It was obvious that her daughter, Libby, wanted to set me up with Marcus because we were both black. I mean the girl was only twelve years old. She knew nothing about me and nothing about Marcus. The only thing she knew was that we would make a cute couple together as she had said over and over again. We were two good-looking black people around the same age. And that was enough. I couldn't fault her for it. Libby was, in fact, doing the same thing I had done when I was her age.

In sixth grade we had three new teachers, all pretty young and close in age: Mr. Davis, Ms. Harris, and Mr. Wilson. Mr. Davis was big and burly. He looked like the heavyweight champion of the world, or at least, our world. Ms. Harris was petite with long, bushy black hair. Both Mr. Davis and Ms. Harris were black. My first black teachers, in fact. And the girls in my sixth-grade class were determined to set the two of them up. We all agreed they made a cute couple. But what makes a cute couple? In my head, I was thinking—and I was sure everyone else was—they match. They were a cute couple because her likeness was the same as his. No one ever considered setting up Ms. Harris with Mr. Wilson. He was funny and cool, but still, it never crossed our minds. Why? Because Mr. Wilson was white. And Ms. Harris was black. They weren't a match.

In first grade we were taught to identify certain likenesses: which pair is a match; which is a mixed-match. Draw a circle around the two that are similar. That was the right answer.

The two that are different are wrong. I made matches inside my head. I paired people together like it was a homework assignment. Tanner and Bethany were a match. They were both short with blond hair. Justin and Meredith were a match, but theirs was harder to explain. They were about the same height but Justin had dark curly hair and Meredith had long blonde hair. Still, they looked cute together—like the couples on TV. Noah and I matched, but only because I wanted us to. I knew everyone would think that I belonged with Humphrey because we were both black, and Noah belonged with Kelly because they were both Korean. I'm not sure how I adopted that way of thinking at such a young age, but I know I wasn't alone in it.

In middle school I spent my summers going to Musical Theater Arts Camp. I remember one year we did the shows *Meet Me in St. Louis* and *Crazy for You*. On the first day of camp the director had all the girls line up according to height and then all the boys line up according to height. The director wanted to see who was a match. She didn't want to pair a boy and a girl together if the boy was shorter than the girl. I knew I wouldn't match with anyone. I was taller than almost all of the boys *and* I was black. The funny thing was, though, when you matched someone with who they looked like, the couple ended up looking more like brother and sister than boyfriend and girlfriend. In *Meet Me in St. Louis* there were two couples. One couple was tall with blond hair, the other was shorter with dark brown hair. They looked like brother and sister, but still, they were a match.

In truth, I was really flattered that Libby should want to set me up with someone, that she had found a match for me. My friends laughed about it—being set up by a twelve-year-old—but they didn't get it. With Libby, I felt like someone was looking out for me. And that felt really good. *Shit, maybe I should make her my maid of honor.* And, yes, I knew the whole thing was rooted in race. To Libby, Marcus and I were two people with a shared likeness moving through a shared space—her space. What I, and the rest of my sixth-grade class, tried to do with Mr. Davis and Ms. Harris, she and her friends were trying to do with me and Marcus—set us up. Circle the two that are similar. That's the right answer. Or at least that *had been* the right answer. It used to be. Today, if you're a black person dating another black person it almost feels like a cliché. Like I'm wrong to want that. Old-fashioned at the very least. I remember a black guy I used to date once said to me, "I know you're not dating me because I'm black. Just like I'm not dating you because you're black." He was right, of course. It was odd, though, that he felt the need to say it. To clear the air. Still, he and I had a shared experience—our blackness. We moved through the world jumping the same hurdles, overcoming the same obstacles, fighting the same fight. Didn't that count for something? I guess for some that doesn't mean much, but for me it does. I wondered if it did for Marcus.

Libby was constantly trying to take a picture of me to bring to Marcus but I was too quick. I never felt camera ready. Instead she was able to take a screenshot of my Facebook profile pic even though I hadn't accepted her friend request. She told me Marcus had called me cute after he saw my picture. That's all I needed to hear to make the first move. I found Marcus's email on Libby's school website and decided to reach out to him.

Hi Marcus,
It's Melva! I believe you and I have a mutual friend. I've been hearing about you since the start of the school year. You're pretty famous where I come from. Anyway, hope you're enjoying spring break!
Talk soon,
Melva

His response:

> Surprise surprise...lucky me. The Melva. You are by far the most popular woman on campus. So, I officially feel horrible about this slow return. I've been getting slanted eyes from your fan club the past few days (quite the loyal group). I hardly use this email address and don't have access to it off campus...nevertheless, I'm hoping better late than never.
> I believe we have a few mutual, part-time middle school students, part-time matchmaker friends... I'm glad you reached out. Spring break was great. I picked up a new hobby, worked, and took a few day trips to Santa Barbara. How are things on your end? Staying out of trouble I hope....
> Look forward to hearing from you.
> Best,
> Marcus

My response:

> Marcus,
> Happy to hear you had a fun spring break. I went home to visit my family on the East Coast for a few days and got to spend time with my best friend, which was really wonderful. What's this new hobby you picked up? Do tell. I hope our young friends haven't been too hard on you. But you have to give them credit...matchmaking is serious work ;)
> Talk soon,
> Melva

We went back and forth like this for a while. Then things got weird. He asked if he could ask me a few questions. *Breakfast, lunch, or dinner?* And then, *Thanksgiving, New Year's, Halloween, Christmas, Valentine's Day, or Fourth of July?* I thought he was asking me out on a date and wanted me to pick when I wanted to go and what meal I wanted to have, but I was wrong. He was just…asking. The questions continued. *Michael Jackson, Prince, Stevie Wonder, Sade, or Janet?* They were never ending. *Fresh Prince, Cosby Show, In Living Color, or Martin?* In one question, he told me to be careful and to know the answer was important. *Basketball, football, soccer, golf, baseball, tennis, or boxing?* My favorite question was the following: *I realize each occasion calls for a different look but if you had to choose, do you prefer to see your man dressed in jeans and a T-shirt, sweats, a suit, jeans and a button up, or shorts and a wifebeater?* On this I refused to answer. I was fed up. Instead I asked him why all the questions. To which he responded:

I can't give away all my secrets, girl! JK. Let's just say I'm plotting. (With no negative intentions whatsoever). But these seemingly random facts about you will undoubtedly help. Besides, I thought I should ask a few easy questions before getting straight to the car, the couch, the bed, the floor, kitchen counter, in public, on balcony or on top, from the back, bottom or the side? JK. Didn't want to move too fast! Lol.

Weird. Things had officially gotten weird. But I agreed to meet him for brunch in West Hollywood anyway. (*I know, I know.*) And I was sorry I did. He wasn't very talkative. And despite emailing me so many questions, he didn't ask me a single one at brunch. In fact, the only question he did ask was after we had eaten and our table had been cleared.

"Do you want to run out on the check?"

"What?"

"Do you want to run out on the check?"

The guy was an ethics teacher. He couldn't be serious. "Is this like one of those scenarios you put your students in to talk about peer pressure?" I asked. He smiled, shook his head, then asked me again. "Look, I don't know you well enough to tell if you're joking or not."

"I'm not joking," he said. "You leave first. I'll wait a while, and then go out behind you."

Are you fucking kidding me?

"Uh, look," I said. "I'm going to stay here and pay for my food, but you're more than welcome to do what you like." He said nothing but remained seated. The waiter came with the bill. Marcus whipped out his card and handed it over before I had the chance to do the same.

"We can split it," I said. He made a face and the waiter laughed at our back and forth before walking away with Marcus's card. I asked Marcus what was the face about.

"I'm not going to let you pay," he said.

"Oh, really?" I said. "A minute ago you didn't want either one of us to pay."

He ignored this.

When Libby asked about the date the following week, I lied and told her I'd had fun but that Marcus and I were just going to be friends. She was disappointed and tried to dig deeper but I shut it down.

I ran into Marcus a few years later on Tinder, the dating app. On Tinder, you see people's pictures and read their profiles (if they write one), and then you swipe right if you like them and left if you don't. If you swipe right and they swipe right, it's a match. Most of the men I match with are black. My friend Amy always asks to see a picture of the guys I match with, and I feel like she just wants to see whether they're black or not. I feel a little self-conscious that for the most part they are, as if black guys are the only guys I'm into or the only guys who are into me. There aren't very many black guys on Tinder, but if you were to look at my phone you'd think I had matched with every single one of them. Only a fraction of the guys I match with actually message me, and only a fraction of those who message me ask me out on a date. It's very frustrating. I was on the app swiping one night when Marcus's pic popped up. Without thinking, I swiped left. Black he may be, but he and I were not a match.

SINGLE BLACK FEMALE

Technically, I've never been in an interracial relationship. I've dated men outside my race, of course, but my boyfriends—a whopping three of them—have all been black. When I got to college, I was shocked, genuinely shocked, to learn there were guys, good-looking, decent guys—black *and* white—who wanted to sleep with me. My high school experience had left me feeling invisible but also undesirable. I had assumed it was because I was black. In the fourteen years I attended Sewickley Academy I had never known anyone outside my race to have a crush on me.

When I broke up with Rob two years after I graduated from college, I started seeing mostly white guys I had gone to school with. One of them was Luke. The first thing he said to me after we had sex was, "I've never slept with an African American woman before." I immediately started putting my clothes back on. There were too many things wrong with that sentence. The first, his use of the word African American. In most instances, when white people say African American instead of black I assume they're doing it for my benefit, so as not to offend me, even though referring to someone as black is not offensive. And so, in his statement, I recognized his need to not offend, and yet I found his words...offensive. It wasn't offensive that he had never slept with a black woman before. It was offensive that he made *our* first time about *him* sleeping with a black woman. He made it about race.

I knew that Luke had dated outside his race before. He had mentioned an ex-girlfriend who was Indian. I wondered if he had uttered the same words to her? *I've never slept with an Indian woman before.* When he mentioned her again in a later conversation about past partners, he referred to her as "the Indian one." I responded without thinking. "Is that how you're going to refer to me one day? As the black one?" It got pretty tense after that. He thought I was calling him racist. Or at least he reacted as such. I told him I was kidding. He said it didn't sound like I was kidding, and I wasn't, but I assured him I was, just so the discomfort would pass.

Carlos was different. Instead of referring to me as black he referred to himself as black even though he was half white, half Puerto Rican. I took it as an attempt to identify with me. To be closer to me. It happened on two occasions. He was telling me that his hero was his stepdad, a white man who had married his mom and taken on "three black kids" who weren't his own. *Uh, what?* Then he told me a story about cops breaking up a party he had attended and arresting him because he had weed on him. "We were all doing it, but of course I was the only *black* kid there, so they arrested me," he said. *Huh?* And all I could think was, *Why do you keep calling yourself black?* I mean, the boy was brown, but he wasn't black. But for me to say so seemed like…I don't know…like it wasn't my place, but now I'm thinking…of course it was my place, whose else's would it be?

Nick was a white guy I went to school with but didn't know until after graduation. We dated while I was still living in New York. Greg was a white guy I dated in Los Angeles. He and I met at a wine tasting. Both Nick and Greg referred to me, or something about me, something I said or did, as ghetto. I hate when white people use the word ghetto. To me it's how they call out blackness, or their *idea* of blackness. It's how they distinguish themselves and their whiteness. Their self-proclaimed cultural superiority. If something is ghetto, then it's a put-down. And that put-down is rooted in race.

Jack was another white guy I dated in Los Angeles, a filmmaker who went to NYU too. We met through mutual friends. We were talking politics one night in a bar and I mentioned having cousins in Florida who voted for Romney. I had sent them emails encouraging them to vote for Obama but they ignored them. Jack's response was, "Do they hate themselves?" I immediately thought of Rob asking me if I was ashamed of being black, which was essentially the same question, right? Do you hate yourself? All of your friends are white. Do you hate yourself? You date a lot of white guys. Do you hate yourself? You're black and you're not voting for the first black president. Do you hate yourself? Do you hate being black? Black people are not the only ones who vote against their own interests, but since a vote against our own interests also meant, at that time, a vote against the first black president, the question had to be asked. But Jack had no business asking it. Still, I didn't know what to say, so I said nothing at all.

I was in Vegas for my sister's bachelorette party with her two best friends from childhood. We met a group of guys one night from Arizona who insisted on following us around everywhere we went. My sister and I were the only black people in the group. Everyone else was white. At one point one of the guys said to me, "We've never met black girls as pretty as you and your sister." *Is that what passes as a compliment from a white guy?! You're pretty for a black girl?!* If I ever stop being shocked by the shit white people say to me, I might be able to start answering back to their bigotry.

My fear, of course, is marrying a white guy and then finding out one day that he's racist. Not really racist, but sort of racist. The kind of racist who doesn't know he's racist, the kind who makes racist jokes, who says the *N* word while singing along to music. Who thinks because he's married to a black woman he gets a pass, or permission, to say things that are not acceptable. That's my fear. And it's pretty real.

I once heard a white woman, a friend of a friend—I'll

call her Jodi—say how she just wasn't attracted to Indian men. She thought about it for a while and then added Middle Eastern men to the mix too. She might have kept going had I not been sitting by her side. Then, in the same breath she used to generalize an entire race of people, she gave an un-apologetic apology to our mutual friend, a white woman who happened to be married to an Indian man. If my friend was offended you couldn't tell.

Do I really want to waste my time trying to figure out which white guys feel the same way as Jodi and which ones don't? That's a lot of whiteness to have to sift through. Do I really want to waste my time with someone who will undoubtedly say something that rubs me the wrong way or shakes me to my core? Who makes our having sex about sleeping with a black woman? Whose idea of a compliment is "you're pretty for a black girl"? Who calls me ghetto when I say or do something he can't relate to? That's a lot of work.

I heard an Asian woman, another friend of a friend, say she just wasn't interested in dating white men, citing their inability to recognize their own privilege as the reason, and I almost high-fived her. I almost stood up to applaud. I couldn't believe how freely and frankly she spoke. It was so gratifying to hear another person of color say what I was too afraid to say myself.

I'm not opposed to marrying a white guy or any other man outside my race. Really, I'm not. It's much more important to me that I find someone who is loyal and loving. However it's also important to me that the man I marry have an in-terest in the advancement of black people, an awareness of social and racial issues that affect the black community, and a deep understanding of and empathy for the plight of black American life. I need a partner who can support my journey as a black woman. I don't necessarily think I'm more likely to find that in a person of color than in a white person, but ignorance and passivity are part of the problem, and so it's important to me that if I do marry a white guy, he be part of the solution.

Today, when someone asks me what my type is, I pretend I don't have one. Like I need time to think about it. Like thirty-seven years hasn't been enough. Like there isn't a tall, lean, artsy, nerdy black guy living inside my head waiting for me to say, "I do." When in truth, I don't feel secure enough to say what it is I really want. If it's a question of race, *and it always is*, I want to marry a black guy. There. I said it. The truth is I have so many white people in my life. So. Many. White. People. It would be nice to go through life with someone who is black, to marry someone who is black. But I may not—studies have shown—marry at all.

I've heard many theories as to why black women are the population group least likely to marry but none more off-putting than my friend Amy's. "Isn't it part of the culture?" she asked. "Don't grandmothers sometimes raise their grandchildren?"

I stopped talking, hoping she might do the same. It was that question of culture that did it. That shut me down completely. To link unmarried black women to grandmothers raising their grandchildren—a subtle hint that a broken black family was, in fact, cultural and not situational—was what offended me most. Still, I made my excuses for her...*maybe she misspoke...maybe I misunderstood.*

"You might have to marry outside your race," she added, as an afterthought.

I knew I wanted to marry a black guy but I didn't know anyone else did. I had never mentioned it before. I'm not sure why. Maybe I just didn't want to rule anyone out. Or maybe admitting I wanted to marry a tall, lean, artsy, nerdy black guy would only draw light to the fact that I was a tall, lean, artsy, nerdy black woman. And how comfortable was I, really, standing in that light? Then again, I *was* able to bring up the plight of unmarried black women to my white friends on more than one occasion, so who knows, maybe I was more comfortable than I gave myself credit for.

Clearly, the subject of unmarried black women was one I needed to talk about. I'm not sure what I wanted, or what I was looking for. If it was something I wanted to say or something I needed to hear.

When you're an unmarried woman in your thirties there's an ongoing conversation about being an unmarried woman in your thirties. I think more than anything I want my friends to know that the conversation is different for me than it is for them. That's all.

#BlackWivesMatter

SQUAD GOALS

I have two black friends. One I see every day when I look in the mirror (she's a real piece of work, that one). And the other is my sister. My best friends have almost always been white. When I was little I had two imaginary friends and even they were white. The kids I sat next to at lunch and played with at recess were white, and the adults whose dinner parties, barbeques, and birthday celebrations I've attended were white.

I tell myself it's no big deal, that the quality of my friends is more important than the color of my friends. I like the way it sounds. It's powerful and progressive, like something Obama would say. Still, I worry that the lack of black people in my life is a reflection on me and my, well, blackness. I worry that others think the same. In truth, it bothers me that my white friends have more black friends than I do—after all, they have me in their life.

Most of the time I try not to think about it. To do so feels like a betrayal. I love and value my friends. I don't want to dishonor them by suggesting our friendship is in some way insufficient because they're white and I'm black. Still, there is an unmistakable void in my life I'm either working to fill or trying to ignore. I want my world and the people in it to be as diverse as children's programming. I'm longing to experience life with people who share in the same strife and struggle as I do. Even more, I want a friend who is fighting the same fight I am. One who experiences life through the same lens, the same set of social conditions, and the same historical context I wake up with and embody every day. I need someone who can reflect back to me the journey I'm on as a black woman. And I feel really guilty about it. Like I'm cheating on my friends. Or thinking about it, anyway. I'm having an emotional affair with black women I've never met or hardly know. My therapist is the only black woman in my life who isn't related to me. When my previous therapist told me she was relocating, I asked that she refer me to an African American therapist. It felt uncomfortable to ask. Wrong even. My previous therapist, like the four before her, had been white. I thought I might offend her or reveal some unknown bias we would then have to talk about. In the end, it was one of the three things I was most proud of that year, along with doing an August Wilson play and leaving my nanny job. I had wrestled with what to say and how to say it, but when my words finally found themselves, they were met with understanding and warmth. I sensed relief even, or perhaps thankfulness, that I had been the one who suggested it and not her.

I try to be as open and honest as I possibly can with my friends. When race is on my mind I tell those I rely on most. I don't know if this is so much a confession about what I'm really looking for in a friendship—an open and ongoing dialogue about race—or a test to see if they can take it. I struggle mostly on my own, and that struggle is alienating. I'm looking for comfort and companionship those around me seem unable to give. But what I do get from my friends is an open ear. I'm always listened to and I do appreciate that. I can talk about race—and they will listen attentively—but there is a struggle or reluctance to contribute. So instead of the conversation being a dialogue, it's much more a monologue.

Sometimes I think they're on to me. At least my friend Brian is. He often remarks on the absence of gay men in his life. "How can I expect to meet a great guy if all I do is hang out with straight women!" he says. Many times I've heard him swear off straight women entirely. "I'm no longer accepting straight female friends!" he says. I envy his bold declaration. He has reached his full capacity of straight female friendships, and I get it and am happy to have made the cut.

"I'm no longer accepting white female friends," I want to say back to him, but I don't. Society has trained me to think my truth is acceptable only when there is no risk of offending others—particularly white people.

"Can you relate?" he asks, and a part of me draws inward. I know he senses this absence of admission.

"Well, yeah, I mean, I'd like to meet a great black guy one day," I admit, uncomfortably aware that this is the first time I've said these words out loud to anyone ever.

"Exactly," he answers back. "Well, that's not going to happen if you keep hanging out with preppy white people."

He's right, of course.

I need to implement my own affirmative action program for allowing people into my life. Or create a vision board with pictures of black people on it, not celebrities, just everyday black people doing everyday things, like buying groceries or walking the dog. I can download pictures online, print them out, and then pin them up on my wall or refrigerator, and hope that the Universe might take the hint.

I was at a house party in Hollywood, scanning the scene, searching for my future husband. I was there by accident. I had run into a guy I took an improv class with. He and his friend were on their way to a nearby party and they insisted I come along. I was feeling pretty spontaneous and so I did. The place was packed with skinny white guys with overgrown beards in vintage T-shirts. I spotted four black people—*four*—two men and two women, mingling with guests. Was it a mirage? Was I so starved for the presence of black people in my life that I'd started imagining them in social settings? The only time I'm in a room with more than two black people is when I'm at home with my family, at church, or getting my hair done. I wanted to befriend each of them. I wanted to ditch the white people I'd shown up with and immerse myself in their company. I found myself standing alone in the corner, sipping on my drink, shooting surreptitious looks their way. I was like a child waiting for a friend to come out to play. After a few long minutes, one of the men made his way over to me. I pretended not to notice or to look too pleased with myself. He stood by my side, smiled, and then spoke. "There's a lot of black people here." It was the first thing out of his mouth, and I was grateful for it.

"I know," I blurted out, unable to stop myself. "I was thinking the same thing."

"I'm usually the only one," he said.

"Me too," I blurted out again, smiling over our shared social status. He didn't seem to notice my enthusiasm, though. He was too busy taking in our surroundings. I decided to do the same. It was like our standing side by side, sharing the same space in a predominantly white place, deserved a moment of silence.

"I had no idea Zack had so many black friends," he said after a while.

"Who's Zack?" I asked.

"The guy whose party it is."

Oh good, I thought to myself, now I know who to be jealous of.

A couple of years ago a young black woman named Melissa moved into my building. She seemed to have met more people in her first four days than I had in the four years I'd lived there. I knew this because of the number of people who began to mistake me for her.

"It's Melissa, right?"

"Hey, Melissa!"

"How's the new place, Melissa?"

It used to be I could check my mail and take out my garbage with complete anonymity. Now I have to, like, make an effort.

"No, it's Melva, actually." I say back to them. They stare at me horror-struck as they come to realize there is more than one young black woman living in the building. I see such shame on their faces that a part of me is tempted to play along. I want to say, "Kidding! Kidding! I'm Melissa!" just to put them out of their misery.

I once attended an audition where the casting director mistook me for the monitor—the person who manages the actors outside of the audition room. The man who auditioned before me had stormed out visibly upset. I waited five seconds or so before going in, and when I did, the casting director had the temperament I was hoping to achieve in my monologue. "If you see the man who just walked out will you please tell him it was not my phone going off but the timer. He was way over two minutes."

"Oh, sure," I said somewhat confused. I began to introduce myself, but she stopped me when she saw my headshot on the top of the stack.

"You're Melva," she said in a meek voice.

"Yes," I said.

"I apologize...I apologize."

"That's okay."

Sitting silently in the room was a piano accompanist. She seemed to be absorbing the discomfort as well, her face turning back and forth between the two of us.

"I apologize...I apologize," she said again.

"It's fine, really."

She apologized two more times before I started my audition piece.

164

The worst, though, was being flagged down in a New York City restaurant where I was having brunch with Mom, having been mistaken for the hostess.

"Can you find our waiter, please?" said an older white woman as I passed by her table.

"Uh, I don't know who your waiter is," I said, "and I don't work here," I added sharply. I lingered just long enough to let my words land. It wasn't her face but the ones around her that grabbed my attention. The two young women across from her, possibly her daughters, looked to be my age and were absolutely mortified.

I've been mistaken for Naomis and Nicoles, Tanyas and Tashas, Monicas, Moniques, and more. If only I could befriend the black women I've been mistaken for. I feel a bond with these women. Like we're tethered together. Like we're moving through the same space, but we keep missing one another. It makes me wonder…who out there is being mistaken for me? Is she the only black person in the room, too? Does she leave that room feeling more alone than when she entered, asking herself, both irritated and intrigued, "Who is this Melva chick?" And then, perhaps, "I wonder what she's like."[6]

---

[6] Update: I've made three black friends since writing this essay. I'm very pleased about that.

'THE HELP' REVISITED

Parents aren't allowed to have favorites, but nannies are. When you're a nanny the kids are like your co-workers, and whichever one is helping you out the most or causing you the least amount of stress is your favorite. Madeline and Morgan were my favorites. Madeline was thirteen. One day we were sitting at an outdoor café on the Promenade in Santa Monica, and she threw her head back and shouted, "I can't wait!" As she chomped on her tuna melt sandwich with a big smile on her face, I asked, "To do what?" "To grow up!" she said with her mouth half full.

Morgan was ten. She was a tomboy, hated surprises, liked to sleep in the clothes she wore to school, and to play her cello while lying on the floor. She'd spend the afternoon yelling at Madeline, arguing that it was her turn to sleep with the cat. Then at night she'd sneak into Madeline's bed, and I'd hear the two of them giggling. With the bedroom door cracked open, I'd peek inside and see their cat curled up between them.

Madeline had two best friends she'd known since she was a baby. Chloe lived across the street and Libby (the matchmaker) around the corner. I was as much their nanny as I was Madeline and Morgan's. We couldn't do anything without them. On good days the four girls reminded me of the young ladies from the movie *Now and Then*—fun, full of life, playful, and charming. On bad days they reminded me of the young ladies from Arthur Miller's *The Crucible*, who accused their parents' slave, Tituba, of witchcraft to avoid wrongdoing of their own.

The girls were always walking a fine line between mischief and misdemeanors. One day they were forced to apologize to the family next door after using their pool without permission. They had pools of their own, of course, but decided it would be more fun to go from one house's pool to the next. They called it pool-hopping. Any wrongdoing was, of course, blamed on me. Where was Melva? What was Melva doing? I started to get anxious, worried that one day they might go a step too far.

When I first started working for Madeline and Morgan's parents it was meant to be temporary. Lori, their mom, was returning to work after ten years to do a short stint back in the office and needed a nanny. Madeline and Morgan were overbooked with after-school activities. She needed someone to do the driving and keep everything running smoothly in between, to make sure homework was done, dinner was made, and baths were taken.

At the end of her tenure, having decided to stay at work, she asked me to stay on as well. I said no. I had decided to retire as a nanny and move on to something else, but that didn't last long. A year or two later, I found myself in need of a new job, and Lori found herself in need of a new nanny. And so we reconnected, and I resumed my post as though I had never left.

Lori was so dependent on me she often referred to me as her co-parent when introducing me to guests. I handled all kid- and family-related responsibilities. I ran errands with the kids. I did their grocery shopping on occasion and went to the post office, pharmacy, and dry cleaner's. I'd stay late putting the final touches on science fair projects, proofreading book reports, reviewing vocabulary words, or handwashing a dress so that it could be worn to school the next day. I had never been more involved in someone else's life. The contact list on my phone was filled with the names and numbers of kids, parents, grandparents, teachers, and tutors. Their contacts outnumbered my own.

I was good at my job. So good, in fact, Lori seemed to think I should do it for her friends' families as well. She'd volunteer my help for after-school pickup or arrange a play-date when a child's parent was preoccupied. "Melva could do it… I'll have Melva do it…" I'd hear her say over the phone. She seemed to enjoy having a nanny who was so helpful she was willing to help others (and not get paid extra for it). In the summer I'd arrive to work with six kids waiting for me to take them to Santa Monica Pier or Universal Studios. It was as if I was working in a fancy foster home for rich white kids. What was troubling was that I enjoyed it. I really did. I felt needed and necessary. And yet, I had come to resent domestic service and my role as a caregiver. I was constant-ly at odds with the long-standing history of black women working for white families, raising their children, managing their households. In America, domestic service is rooted in race. It's part of our history. As a black nanny I had to hold that history every day and confront it from within. I felt like Viola Davis and Octavia Spencer in *The Help*. I constantly had to remind myself that it was different. It wasn't 1960 and it wasn't Jackson, Mississippi. For starters, I could use the same bathroom the family used. I didn't have to go to an outhouse in the back of the yard. I was also expected to sit down and eat with them during meals. Still, I could not escape the servile nature of my position, particularly Lori's tendency to lend my services to those in need of them. I felt like I had no agency.

There's a scene in *The Help* that has always felt a little too familiar to me. In the scene, Skeeter, played by Emma Stone, asks her friend Elizabeth if her maid Aibileen, played by Viola Davis, can help her with a job she has to do for work. "*My* Aibileen," her friend says.[7] Reluctant at first, Elizabeth

---

[7] Taylor, Tate, and Ahna O'Reilly. *The Help*. Showtime Anytime streaming service. Directed by Tate Taylor. Burbank, CA: Walt Disney Studios Motion Pictures, 2011.

agrees when she learns Skeeter's maid has left her. Later, after Skeeter and Aibileen begin working together, Elizabeth says, without warning, that the arrangement is off. Skeeter will have to find help somewhere else. I always sensed that Lori, like Elizabeth, had this feeling of ownership over me, and that if others wanted to hire me, they had to go through her. But if someone needed my help then they should have asked me themselves. I'm my own person.

One of Lori's friends felt the need to explain why she asked for Lori's permission first. "My female friendships mean the world to me," she said. "I don't want to do anything to upset them." And so, out of respect, she'd spoken to Lori before speaking to me. But what about respect for me? In time, friends of Lori did come to me first. And Lori admitted to me one day that she didn't really like it when her friends and other parents at school asked me to babysit or help out while I was watching her kids or when I wasn't watching her kids for that matter. That was news to me. Only when they went to her first did it seem acceptable.

When Lori's friend Joan (the matchmaker's mother who had never dated a black guy) offered to take Madeline and Morgan on summer vacation with her daughter, Libby, she assumed I would join them to help out. I finally had to put my foot down. It was a difficult phone call to make. "I don't work for Joan," I told Lori. "If Joan needs my help then Joan needs to pay me." The conversation went better than I anticipated. There were a couple of rough patches along the way, but we finally got on the same page. In the end, Lori understood. And I was reminded that along with sharing a bathroom and being invited to dinner, I could say no. I could have boundaries. I could stand up for myself. Something my predecessors never could.

When it came to issues of race, Lori had taken me by surprise. Chloe's mom, Karen, planned to take the girls to get their nails done the day before school started. Apparently, it was a tradition. But when Madeline asked to go, Lori had said no. She said she didn't like the idea of four little white girls being pampered by a staff of Asian women. She thought it spoiled them and set a poor precedent. I was struck by her racial attentiveness. That she was actively trying to counter a culture in which women of color catered to white women and girls. Of course, this was someone's livelihood so her method might have been misguided. But in the end, she gave in.

One day I walked into Lori and Mike's room where Madeline was doing her homework and Lori was recovering from a cold, and I heard this: "Don't say that! It's not funny. It's racist." Lori was yelling at Madeline, who was laughing. I had forgotten why I was there and turned to leave, not wanting to be a part of the conversation, not wanting to witness one more word of it, not wanting to have to stand up for black people everywhere or to be put in a position to do something, say something. On my way out I heard Lori say, "The reason why Asian people are smarter than us is because they work hard and study." And Madeline's giggles subsided.

Lori condemning her daughter's racist joke was a bit of a role reversal. Months earlier Lori had been packing up some of the girls' toys to give to Miriam, their housekeeper. It struck me as odd, because Miriam was around my age and had no children of her own. I asked why she was giving the toys to Miriam and she said she might know someone with kids. In response to the odd expression on my face she said, "She's Mexican. All they do is have babies."

And then it was Madeline's turn to speak up. "Mom that's racist."

Morgan chimed in, too. "Yeah, mom, that's racist."

It should have been reassuring, Madeline and Morgan's willingness to speak up the way that they had, and, in part, it was. But not entirely. When a Macklemore song came on the radio in the car, Morgan said he sounded black and was surprised to learn that he was actually white. When I challenged her on this, asking what a black person sounded like, she got frustrated and said, "Never mind." I already knew, though, what she thought black people sounded like. Morgan used to go around the house mocking the "Ain't Nobody Got Time for That" viral YouTube video in a voice that made me cringe. And upon hearing an ethnic-sounding name, she'd scoff and say how weird it was. I just hoped she'd never be put in a position one day to review someone's resume. "What kind of name is Lakeisha?" she might say. "What kind of name is Lamar? Next!" And then there was Madeline. We were driving along Sunset one evening when Kanye's "All of the Lights" came on the radio. She started singing along, and I almost pulled the car over when I heard her say the *N* word.

"Do not use that word!" I snapped.

"I'm sorry, I'm sorry, I'm sorry," she said hurriedly.

"You're repeating words you don't understand," I continued, trying to maintain control over the steering wheel and my temper. "There is an entire history behind that word that you know nothing about."

"I'm sorry, I'm sorry, I'm sorry," she said again.

Her reaction told me that she did, in fact, know better. Maybe it had just slipped out. Or maybe she thought she could get away with it. I don't know.

Later, at Madeline's bat mitzvah, I heard fifty white kids shout the *N* word while singing along to Kanye and Jay-Z's "Niggas in Paris." No one seemed to notice but me. I was standing on the sidelines, sipping my ginger ale (too timid to enjoy an alcoholic beverage with my employers) when the familiar beat dropped, and a stampede of awkward adolescents stormed the dance floor.

I was the only black person over the age of thirteen in the

room. There were maybe four black kids. And I couldn't help but wonder what they might be feeling. I wanted to unplug the sound system, grab the microphone, and make it a teachable moment. But I didn't. I stayed in my spot, making casual conversation with Madeline's Hebrew teacher and writing a strongly worded letter to the hip-hop moguls in my head.

Dear Kanye and Jay-Z,
I want you to stop using the N word so the white kids I nanny for will stop using it too. I know your music isn't made or meant for them but they don't. They're white. They think everything was made and meant for them. I've endured a lot as a nanny—a lot—but teaching white kids why they can't use the N word is above my pay grade.
Sincerely,
Melva

When I first interviewed for the position, I told Lori I was a writer and an actress. I had just finished writing an original TV pilot, which she offered to read. She told me she had connections to TV writers, and that they might be able to help me out. Many of the families I worked for in the past had connections to the entertainment industry, yet none other than Lori had offered to help my career. I was stunned.

A few months after I started working for her, I applied to a writing fellowship at a TV network and needed a recommendation from an agent or industry professional. As I didn't have an agent at the time, I decided to ask Lori if she knew anyone who would be willing to read my work and write me a recommendation. She said she'd ask. She did and one agreed. I couldn't believe how very helpful everyone was being. I was so thankful, so appreciative, and I began to think maybe this new nanny job would mark the end of my nanny career and the beginning of something else, something more.

A couple of years later, after I returned to work for Lori

for the second time, she was working on her computer, re-viewing a trailer for a movie she was working on. Both she and her husband, Mike, worked behind the scenes in the entertainment industry. I was bustling in the kitchen when Lori was suddenly struck with an idea. "That's what you should do," she said to me. "Copywriting. You could do this." Within days Lori started training me as a copywriter. Again, I couldn't believe how helpful she was. Copywriting was new to me, but I picked it up quickly. I enjoyed doing it, and I was good at it. Lori thought so, too. She seemed set to hire me as a copywriter on an upcoming project until a sudden shift occurred. She told me of a conversation she'd had with Mike.

"Who did the grocery shopping?" Mike had asked.

"Melva saw the list I left for Miriam. She knew Miriam hadn't come in today and did it herself. She also made dinner," Lori had said.

"I hope she isn't any good at copywriting," Mike had said.

From then on Lori's attitude about my copywriting career changed.

"You better not leave me when you start making money as a copywriter," she'd say. "I will blacklist you." I laughed but didn't find it at all funny. Lori started communicating with me less and less about copywriting. When I brought it up to her one day over the phone, she said she wasn't really in a position to offer me anything. That was more Mike's territory, and he was really busy at the moment. Something had changed, and I knew why—she didn't want to lose me as her nanny. She had realized she was acting against her own interest and put a stop to it. In fact, she made a comment about my working for her until Morgan went to college— eight years away—and I knew then we weren't on the same page. I was disappointed but not surprised. The idea that a family I was working for might help me succeed was a little too good to be true. It was much more convenient for her to keep me in my place.

I was in Lori's office one day dropping the girls off when she held up a movie poster and asked for my opinion. "What do you think?" she asked. "We're trying to reach a more *urban* crowd." Then she laughed and said, "You're the least urban person I know."

Urban is code for black. It can be found in the lexicon for Language White People Use to Discuss Black People—right after *thug*. I know all the code words. One time I was sitting in the lobby outside my acting class, preparing for a scene I had to do, when a woman I had never met before came up to me and asked, "What's another word for ghetto?" She whispered the last word, as if she didn't want anyone to hear her using it. "Uh, inner city? Urban?" I said, and her eyes lit up with recognition. "Thank you," she said gratefully.

"So what do you think?" Lori pressed on, holding up the proposed movie poster, "These are supposed to be *your* people."

My people.

Supposed to be.

My people.

If there is a proper comeback to the degradation of one's self, I don't know what it is. The worst part is that I had to continue showing up for her. I had to work for a woman who saw me as an outlier of my race—if she saw me at all. I mean, really. What's the point of having a black nanny if she can't help her white boss reach a more urban market for work? I told her the poster was fine. I didn't want to participate in her game of "How Black Is My Black Nanny?" with its host, "I Don't Know I'm Being Racist." I've been a contestant on that show and others like it too many times and I always leave empty-handed. I can't win.

One of the hardest parts of being a nanny was negotiating my salary. It was often the breaking point in an otherwise civil relationship. Many parents gave me a hard time for it. One mother said she appreciated my wanting to earn twenty dollars an hour but it just wasn't realistic. She had three boys, by the way. Three of them. I had an urge to say *I appreciate your wanting to pay fifteen dollars an hour but it's just not realistic.* I once ended up doing an odd job for a woman in Bel Air, writing thank you cards at the desk in her den. It took me three hours to do it. I asked for fifty dollars. She was shocked by this and wanted to pay me forty-five. "I don't even pay my housekeeper that much," she said. Like her housekeeper has anything to do with me. When I insisted on fifty, she said, "Do you have anything else to be doing right now?" I laughed. I couldn't help it. That woman thought so little of me and my time.

"I have a lot of things I could be doing right now," I said. "None of them pay," I admitted. "But they still need to get done." In the end, she paid me the fifty dollars.

No one wants to be taken advantage of. I get that. And I suppose, because both those women lived in Bel Air, they probably thought that I thought they had money to spare. But what I was asking for had nothing to do with them and everything to do with me. My salary requirement was not based on what I thought of their wealth. It was based entirely on the job demands and what I knew I was worth.

I've never left a job because of the kids. It was always because of the parents. Lori and I had a falling out. I sent her an email asking to be reimbursed for gas. The driving was out of control. There were after-school activities, the movies, the pier, the promenade, Universal Studios, and friends' houses, which were located throughout the city. She responded by saying we needed to have a conversation about money. And we did. It didn't go well. It was horrible, in fact. It got very heated. I'm not sure why. Actually, I do know why. She took everything I said personally. And I took everything she said personally. "I can't believe you think you're entitled to more money," she said to me.

My temper rose and I tried to keep it as simple and straightforward as I could. "I don't think I should be responsible for gas when I'm driving Madeline and Morgan and all of their friends around town," I said.

Lori seemed to think she was paying me enough to cover gas and whatever help she needed on the weekends. "I was really hurt," she added, "when you asked to be paid to work weekends."

I was dumbfounded. That's what employers do. They pay their employees for work. I'm not a family friend who can do free favors. Who's entitled now?

When the conversation ended, nothing was resolved. Lori kept using the word entitled, which was getting under my skin. Entitled is the word you use when you think people are not deserving of what they have or what they ask for. When she spoke to me, the subtext was always the same. *How dare you ask me for more money? How dare you? How dare you? How dare you?*

I gave my notice. I couldn't work for someone who didn't think I was worth what I was getting paid. I knew it would only create tension, a poor work environment, and it would continue to come up again and again. Three days after I gave notice, she found someone new to replace me. I was driving to work when she called and told me it would be my last day. I was pissed, thinking I had two more weeks of pay, but I held it in and said okay. I took the girls and two of their friends to Santa Monica Pier one last time. We walked along the boardwalk, went on rides, and then sat on the beach. When we got back to the house, Lori called and suggested a compromise—stay until the end of the week. I refused.

"So you're unwilling to compromise?" she said.

"You told me today was my last day so today is my last day," I said. Presumably, the scheduling with her new nanny had backfired and she needed me for another week, but I felt like I was being toyed with. Me, my salary, my livelihood were all being toyed with. I wanted it to end, so I ended it.

I didn't see Lori before I left, and I didn't want to. I dropped Morgan off at one of her lessons and left Madeline at home as usual. A week later I sent Lori an email reminding her of what she owed me. She replied with a very heated response. She called my rate "absurd" and suddenly took issue with my work as her nanny. She concluded her email with this: "I am in awe of your sense of entitlement. I thought you were decent and generous, but I feel truly victimized by your approach to this matter."

There's a line in *The Help* where Skeeter's maid Constantine, played by Cicely Tyson, says, "Every day you're not dead in the ground, when you wake up in the morning, you gonna have to make some decisions. You gotta ask yourself this question, 'Am I gonna to believe all them bad things that fools say about me today? Am I gonna believe all them bad things fools say about me today.'"[8] After reading Lori's email I had to make that very decision.

I needed to cool off, so I waited a day and a half before I responded. I didn't want to write a response that was reactionary, pure emotion. In the end, I wrote two emails but I sent only one. One was for me and one was for her. The first was what I wanted to say. The second was what I needed to say. I sent the second. It said the following:

> I understand the need to process your emotions, but this process has nothing to do with me. You have made continued efforts to make a business-related issue into

---

[8] Taylor, Tate, and Cicely Tyson. *The Help*. Showtime Anytime streaming service. Directed by Tate Taylor. Burbank, CA: Walt Disney Studio Motion Pictures, 2011.

a personal one. This is both inappropriate and unpro-
fessional. You continue to delay, or refuse, payment for
childcare services you received. You have chosen this
moment to express dissatisfaction with my job performance, and have made assertions that are inaccurate
and at this point irrelevant, while I continue to depend
on the money I earned for the work I did....

She responded with another heated email that concluded
with: "I'll ask our lawyer." And I was done. Defeated. I felt
so used. I had spent so much time bending over backwards
for her and her family, only to be disrespected. Disregarded.
Then, an hour and a half later, I received yet another email.

After talking it through I feel the best course is a clean
break. You have been professional and reliable and have
given a lot under challenging circumstances. I'm sorry
that we disagreed on compensation but I remain grateful for the quality of work you have done.

Three weeks later I received a check in the mail.

When you're treated less than, when you have to prove
your worth, when you spend your life moving in and out of
white spaces looking for an ally, longing for an ally, it can be
difficult to know if everyday injustices are because of your
color or your character or both. I'm constantly asking myself:
Would this happen if I were white? Would they look at me
this way, would they speak to me this way, would they treat
me this way if I were white? My relationship with Lori was
civil as long as I was silent. When I spoke up, everything went
to shit. She could ask me for what she needed, but I couldn't
ask her for what I needed. This was a supremacist way of
thinking, one that existed in 1960 in Jackson, Mississippi,
and it still exists today. Lori hadn't wanted to pay me what
she owed me because she was angry. She was angry I could
walk away, and she couldn't do anything about it. Was our

falling-out rooted in race? Or was it just about gas money? America has a history of devaluing not only the lives of black people but also the work we do and the contributions we make. Our bodies were sold to the highest bidder. How do I grapple with my own feelings of worth when my story starts with a price tag on my back? When I entered the workforce I was at an immediate disadvantage because of my race and gender. Black people—black women especially—are not valued as highly as everyone else. Oftentimes we're not seen as equal. We see this in how much black women are paid for doing the same work as everyone else. It's a systemic problem that has seeped into the psyche of both the employer and the employee, whether they be white, black, men, or women. To an employer, society says your black employees are worth less than your white employees, your female employees less than your male employees. Therefore, when I find myself having to fight for what I am owed, I can't help but think that, no, this isn't just about gas money. This is about something much more. This is about who I am and what society says I'm worth. This is about a white woman who called me entitled when I asked to be reimbursed for the gas I was using to drive her children around town. A white woman who called me entitled when I asked that she pay me to work weekends. A white woman who called me entitled when she thought she could avoid paying me the remainder of what she owed me. The tone she took, the language she used, continues to stay with me. The underlying message was crisp and clear to me. *Ungrateful Negro…ungrateful Negro… ungrateful Negro.*

NO JUSTICE, NO PEACE

I had quit my nanny job the week before George Zimmerman went on trial for murder. And good thing too. I don't know how I could have received news of his acquittal and tended to its gross assault on the black psyche while catering to the whims and wishes of two well-off white girls. Don't get me wrong. I was very fond of those two well-off white girls, but when an unarmed black teen is shot dead, domestic service feels like a terrible misuse of my time. So instead of waking up to make meals and arrange playdates, instead of searching for a new nanny position, I plopped on my couch and watched around-the-clock news coverage as if a tropical storm was headed my way.

Watching the trial was my way of showing up for Trayvon in a way I hadn't before. When he was killed, I remained decidedly distant, too overwhelmed by the magnitude of his murder to fully take it in. I remember admitting to a friend that I wasn't giving him enough of my time and attention. And it was true. I wasn't. But now I was ready to mourn him and everything he stood for. Ready to give him all of my time, all of my attention.

The entire trial was a case against blackness or otherness. It justified racial profiling and the ideas of anyone who has crossed the street, held on to their purse, or locked their car doors. What happened to Trayvon Martin reaffirmed a core belief, a core wound that has lived inside me since I was six years old: being black means you don't belong. Intellectually, I know that's not true. In my heart, I know that's not true. Still, I can't ignore the evidence and experience I've had that says otherwise. A grown man carrying a gun saw a black teenage boy alone on a sidewalk and for no reason, no justification, other than the color of his skin, decided the boy was a threat, that he was up to no good, that he didn't belong, and the grown man chose to follow the boy in a pursuit that would end the boy's life. And I'm full of pain and an unspeakable sorrow, because what happened to Trayvon happens again and again and again.

When the verdict was announced I called Mom first. "I'm sick. Just sick," she said. Then I called my friend Amy. I was expecting her voicemail but was pleasantly surprised when she picked up. Amy wasn't a phone person. She was also working from home, but she stayed on the phone with me for over an hour. The next day I asked her to accompany me to a Justice for Trayvon Martin rally. When she declined, I felt the sting of disappointment. Then I called Jordan, the only black person I was in touch with at the time (outside of my family). Jordan and I had met in college. He was Rob's old roommate. We were both living in Los Angeles now and had recently reconnected. Like Rob, Jordan and I had long phone conversations about race and racism. Like Rob, Jordan and I were never on the same page. Like Rob, Jordan liked to call me innocent and naïve, oblivious to what was really going on. That what I knew to be true was only half the story. I'd get off the phone feeling angry and resentful. But I already *was* angry and resentful, so I called him. No answer. I stewed in silence before drifting off to sleep.

The next day I attended the Justice for Trayvon Martin rally in East Los Angeles. It was my first protest. I thought it might relieve my overwhelming grief. I thought it might connect me to my community. Somewhere in the back of my mind, though, I thought I might meet someone. Like *the* one. *There are going to be so many black guys at this rally,* said a voice inside my head, and I couldn't help but feel uplifted, if only a little, imagining hundreds of eligible black men filling the streets of East Los Angeles fighting for justice while simultaneously looking for their better half. Who knew, I thought. I might find myself standing beside a smart, self-aware, emotionally mature, handsome young black man. Amid chants of "No Justice, No Peace," he'll nudge me on the shoulder, smile, and say, "You wanna get outta here?" And then from there, who knew!

When I got to the rally I scanned the scene, the same way I do when I go to a party, a bar, or a restaurant, and in doing so felt a surge of shame. *This isn't what I'm here for,* I thought. *This isn't what I came here to do.* I made my way through the crowd. The turnout was only okay. There were a lot of families. Little ones holding the hands of mothers and fathers. There was a shrine with candles, flowers, and a picture of Trayvon. Tables were set up with poster boards, stencils, and spray paint to make signs. I didn't really feel like doing an arts and crafts project, but it seemed I had to. When I finished my sign, I took my place among the crowd that stood on the curb of the sidewalk and shouted, "No justice, no peace!" A long line of police officers stood on the block opposite us, armed and ready. I was insulted by their presence. Cars drove by honking their horns, and we cheered in appreciation before returning to our chant. I tried to raise my voice to match the ones around me, who shouted at the top of their lungs, their fury and frustration evident in every word, every syllable, but I couldn't do it. I didn't have the energy. I had expended it all the night before when I learned of the news.

The rally wasn't what I had imagined. I thought I'd feel energized, emboldened. Instead I just felt exhausted. I stood on the sidewalk, holding my sign, noticing passersby going on about their day. I envied them. I thought of all the times I'd walked past protesters in Union Square in New York, unaware and unburdened. The chant continued, "No justice, no peace! No justice, no peace!" I said it over and over again until my emotional dam broke and tears fell from my eyes.

"Are you okay?" asked the person standing next to me. She wasn't the smart, self-aware, emotionally mature, handsome young black man I had hoped for but instead a tiny white woman with a round face and very short dark brown hair.

"Yeah," I said, embarrassed, trying to hold back more tears. "It's just a lot."

"I know," she said softly.

Did she, though? I let her talk while I composed myself. She told me of some organization she was a part of and gave me a news article to read. I listened to her for several long minutes, then returned to the chants of the crowd now ringing in my ears. A voice inside my head asked, *So how long are we going to do this?*

Nothing felt right. Not the setting. Not the chanting. Not the police staring back at me. Not the sign I was holding. I kept thinking this isn't me. *But this is activism. But it still isn't me. I'm not a protester. How can I protest when my grief outweighs my anger? How can I engage when I find the whole thing pointless?* And I did. I felt another surge of shame. What if the protesters of the Civil Rights era felt the same way? Where would I be then? Did they ever feel it was all pointless? Probably not.

I drove home feeling disappointed in myself. I entered my apartment feeling more miserable than when I left. I saw evidence of hopefulness scattered throughout—change of clothes thrown everywhere, makeup all over my vanity area. I had actually thought I might meet someone. Like *the one.* Someone to share my space with, my pain with. When I told my friends this they laughed. It was amusing to them. I get it. I joined in and laughed, too. Did I really go to a Trayvon Martin rally thinking I might meet a guy? What does that say about me? Oh, I know. It says I'm lonely as fuck.

I slid off my shoes, took a deep breath, and returned to my bed.

The woman I met at the rally found me on social media and we became friends on Facebook. She invited me to a meeting her organization was holding. She followed up by posting a message to my timeline.

Hi Melva,

It was really good meeting you at the Justice for Trayvon Martin protest in Boyle Heights. I wanted to invite you to this panel happening at Chuco's Justice Center in Inglewood on Thursday night. There will be speakers from several organizations talking about how we can fight the New Jim Crow and stop the criminalization of youth. Hope you can make it! Let me know if you have any questions.

I didn't respond. I didn't show up.

The rally revealed something new about me that I was sorry to learn. Activism doesn't really look good on me. But what is activism? Is it standing on a street corner shouting and holding up signs? Is it a raised fist in the air? Is it aggressive Facebook posts? I suppose it is for some, but I don't think it is for me.

What does activism look like on me?

Not this, I thought. Not this.

THE NEIGHBORHOOD WATCH

I was home visiting Mom and Dad in Sewickley, and as I walked through town I spotted a Neighborhood Watch sign. I never used to notice Neighborhood Watch signs. The sign had new meaning for me since the death of Trayvon Martin. I wondered if it was a new addition to the neighborhood or if signs like that had always populated the town. I stopped to stare at it. What does suspicious activity look like, I wondered? And who exactly was doing the watching? Was it all the people whose eyes I felt upon me as I walked in and out of stores, up and down the street?

When I'm in Sewickley and I feel a person looking at me, I want to turn around and say, "I grew up here. This is my home. This is my hometown." Afterwards, I'm struck with sadness. Why do I always feel I have to prove myself wherever I go, wherever I am? I have a right to be wherever I stand.

I took a moment to remember Trayvon. I thought about how scared he must have been the night he lost his life. I tore my eyes away from the sign and continued my walk, fighting the feeling I'd felt since I arrived; I no longer felt at home in my hometown.

When Mom and Dad were renovating the house they currently live in, Mom stopped by the house midday and found the neighbors, the ones who lived on either side of them, in their would-be mudroom having a conversation. Years later, a man who lived across the street from my parents walked onto their property to take a look at their pond and the work that was being done to their backyard. I was home visiting. It was an early summer morning, and I was on the other side of the house, outside on the patio so I didn't see him. I only knew about it because the man told Dad he'd been in our yard and Dad told me. I was stunned. His actions were the whitest, most privilege bullshit there is. Who but a white man is confident enough, feels safe enough, to trespass on someone else's property for no other reason than to look at the work they are doing on their yard? If you're black, that shit will get you shot. Mom can't step into a home that's being renovated to see the work that's being done on it. Dad can't walk into someone's backyard bright and early in the morning to check out the landscaping. They can't walk onto someone else's property as if it's their own. They can't be nosy. You can't do those things when you're black. You just can't. And the fact that my parents' neighbors don't stop to consider that what they are doing might not be okay with my parents is maddening.

Dad was very gracious about the man's intrusion. He told him the next time he would like to take a look at his yard, just knock on the door and ask. The man said okay. I was in disbelief. I still am.

When it comes to the Neighborhood Watch, the neighborhood is white America and all eyes are on us.

I had a run-in with a neighbor when I was living in New York. I was walking home from the grocery store and was a few feet from the front door when a man entered the building ahead of me. I caught the door before it closed, thankful I wouldn't have to put my groceries down and dig for my keys just yet. The man had seen me rushing to the door but made no effort to hold it open for me. I followed him into the entryway and headed to the elevator, a few steps behind him, when he stopped and turned to me. "Do you live here?" he asked.

"Excuse me?" I said. I was carrying two bags of groceries. Who did he think I was? *Delivery?*

"Do you live here?" he repeated.

"Do you?" I asked.

"Yes," he answered. "I'm in apartment 5A."

I hesitated a moment. "I don't usually tell people I don't know where I live," I said.

"Look," he said, holding his ground, blocking my path to the elevators. "I have a right to know if the people who are entering my building live in it or not."

His building—oh, okay.

"Well," I said, my temper rising, voice shaking, "I'll tell you what, you can either stand there and watch as I search for my keys to check my mail or you can follow me as I ride the elevator up to my floor and enter my apartment. Your choice." I squeezed passed the man and continued to the mailboxes.

"You know, there's no need to get an attitude," he said, before making his way up the stairs.

Attitude. It's code for black. I know all the code words, remember? *Attitude* can be found in the lexicon for Language White People Use to Discuss Black People—right after *angry*. It's a word reserved for black women who stand up for themselves, speak up for themselves, or, to put it another way, black women who are being "difficult." I was fuming. First, this white man was trying to police my actions. *Then,* he was trying to police my emotions. If he had said hello, if he had introduced himself, I would have done the same. I would have said, "Nice to meet you, 5A, I'm Melva, I'm in apartment 4D." It could have been that simple, that civilized. Instead he stopped to question me. What gave him the right to do that? To him, I was somewhere I wasn't supposed to be. I didn't belong. And it was his job to remind me.

If you see something, say something—right? I used to think these words were *for* me and now I know they're *about* me.

In college I went on a trip to Disney World with my best

friend and her family. A store clerk at one of the boutiques in the Magic Kingdom asked me if I was going to pay for the light-up Minnie Mouse thingamajig I was holding in my hand. I told her I had paid for it. They sold the light up thingamajig in every store at every stand throughout the park. I hadn't bought it at that particular store, but I had indeed bought it. She didn't believe me, though. I could tell by the look on her face. She thought I had stolen it. She thought I was a shoplifter. I'm sure customers come in carrying store items bought at other locations all the time. It's Disney World. They sell the same shit at every stand in every store. Does she stop to question all of them? Somehow, I think not. Suddenly the happiest place on earth had become the whitest place on earth. And I was trespassing.

I was on vacation with my parents in New Orleans. This was after I had moved to Los Angeles. It was our first time staying at a Ritz Carlton hotel, and although the suite I was sharing with Mom and Dad didn't afford me the privacy I had hoped for, the hotel was otherwise pleasant to stay in. We'd had a full day of touring a plantation and walking through slave cabins, and we were happy to return to the hotel. The elevator was almost full, but we squeezed into it. I noticed a short white woman with short black hair taking us in as we made room for ourselves. When the elevator arrived at our floor we let the woman off first. We walked behind her, discussing dinner plans for the evening, and I noticed Mom glance at the woman and then back at me and then make a face that only Dad and I could see.

We continued walking down the hallway and I saw what Mom had noticed. Every other step, the woman snapped her head back to look at us, as if checking to see if we were still behind her. She picked up her pace and when she reached her room, she pressed herself up against the door and looked at us with an expression of fear on her face, as if to say, "Please

God, don't hurt me!" My parents and I continued to walk on by.

How can I be comfortable, confident in the skin I'm in when the skin I'm in incites fear, suspicion, apprehension, even violence in others? How can I be bold and brave in my skin when I have to defend it, when I'm constantly shamed for it? When its color—my color—holds a horrible and hateful history—a history that lives on to this day, a history that others still cling to, a history immortalized by monuments that others refuse to take down? How am I to move through the world with my head held high, moving in and out of spaces like I belong, like I'm supposed to be wherever I am, without looking down at the ground? An acting teacher I had in Los Angeles called me out on it. "I see you, Melva," she said, "as someone who doesn't like to take up a lot of space. Me? When I walk into a room? I take up as much space as I can." I didn't tell her that when she, a white woman, walks into a room people make space for her. They step aside without her even knowing it. I didn't tell her that when I, a black woman, walk into a room, I have to subject myself— my blackness—to scrutiny or surrender the space I'm in. I didn't tell her that I don't take up space because it's not safe for me to do so. I didn't tell her that in that very moment, as I sat in class, with everyone's eyes upon me, with everyone casually musing over why Melva doesn't like to take up space, I was shrinking. I didn't tell her that as a black woman in white America I've been told, I've been taught, implicitly if not explicitly, that the space I'm in doesn't really belong to me, that I have it on loan from white people, and they can usurp it at any time.

SHIT WHITE PEOPLE SAY ABOUT BLACK PEOPLE

I was driving back to Los Angeles from an audition I'd had in San Diego, and I was listening to the latest episode of my friend Brian's podcast. He's a comedy writer and his co-host, Jodi (the friend of a friend who just wasn't attracted to Indian men), a standup comedian. Their guest, Kimmy, was also a standup comedian who, like Jodi, had just done a show in Oakland, California. "Can we just say," Jodi began, as I listened behind the steering wheel of my Mini Cooper, "for this gig, and I would say this if there were black people in this room right now, it was a lot of black people—"

"There was not a white person in the audience," Kimmy added.

"The audience was all black," Jodi continued, "and when you're a white girl it can be intimidating."

As soon as I heard "I would say this if there were black people in this room right now," I knew that what would follow would not be good. My heart sank. It was like I was listening to a friend talk about me behind my back. To hear that Jodi, someone I knew, someone I've spent time with, even shared Thanksgiving dinner with, was only comfortable with blackness when it came in small doses was not altogether surprising, but it was disappointing. Jodi was fine doing comedy for a group of white people with a few black people in the audience. But a room full of black people intimidated her, or, to use another word, scared her, because that's what intimidation is—fear. That is why when white people say, "I'm not a racist. My best friend is black," it's such bullshit. All that tells me is that you, like Jodi, are comfortable with blackness in very small doses. I walk into white spaces every day. The intimidation I feel is not only based on the micro-aggressions I experienced as a child and as an adult, but it is history itself. Historically speaking, it is unsafe for black people to walk into white spaces. My intimidation, my fear, my discomfort is a very real one. Her fear is false. Her intimidation speaks to the lies that are told about us, the lies that say black people are dangerous.

Jodi and Kimmy went on to say they were the best of the white girls who performed, and that the audience responded more positively to them because they were both considered "safe white." When Brian asked Kimmy to define what "safe white" meant, she said, "We're very like 'we're not going to steal your man white.'" Okay. Stop the tape. Let's say there *is* such a thing as safe white. Safe white is "I'm not going to silence and shame your blackness. I'm going to see you for who you are." Safe white is "I'm going to do the work I need to do to recognize my own implicit bias." Safe white is "When I hear your story, I'm going to believe it." Safe white is "I'm not going to stand by and be silent in the face of racial injustice. I'm going to raise my voice." That's what safe white is...for a start. Kimmy was projecting onto black women a lie she's been told about black women—one that she was now perpetuating. That, to me, is not safe white.

The conversation continued. They talked about how in comedy female comics have to watch what they wear because if they dress too sexy, women in the audience would feel threatened and men in the audience would be turned on. But you don't want to dress too neutral either because then your sexual orientation will be questioned or confused. Kimmy said that she wore combat boots just to be safe because if you're a white girl and you wear heels "those black women" take one look at you and say, "She think she cute." Kimmy said this in a stereotypical black woman's voice.

"I'm glad you did that," said Jodi. "I always get shit for doing a black voice."

Brian, laughing, then urged Jodi to do her stereotypical black woman's voice. "I know you have one, too," he said, "so do yours." And she did.

When I hear a white person do a "black woman's voice" it never sounds like me. Never. It doesn't sound like me. It doesn't sound like Mom. It doesn't sound like my sister. It doesn't sound like my aunts. It doesn't sound like the women I know. So this, yet again, is not only an attack on blackness, it's an example of white people perpetuating an image, an idea of what they think blackness is. To me, a white person doing a stereotypical black voice is a modern minstrel. There is a historical context that needs to be considered. They may not be doing it in blackface, but mimicking or mocking a black person's voice, mannerisms, or behavior is part of the origins of minstrelsy. The intent is the same, and, more importantly, so is the impact.

In almost the same breath Kimmy had used to do her stereotypical black woman's voice, she said that with white comics there's so much variety—her set is so much different than Jodi's—but black comics "all pretty much sound the same." After some insistence from Brian and Jodi, she amended that comment to say that black *urban* comics all sound the same. When relaying the story to my therapist, this is where I started to cry. I think everyone has something to say. I think everyone has a story to tell. And it's disheartening to hear white people write off black artists and black storytellers— because that's what comedians are, storytellers—as all pretty much sounding the same. It's hurtful and hard to hear. This is where the "there can be only one" mentality comes from. White people think black people are all the same and there is no nuance in our experiences or in our stories. And black people know that white people think this, which is why we feel we have to compete with one another for that one spot, that one chance to tell our story. We all have stories that are aching inside of us. And when we get the opportunity to tell them, when we summon the courage, we're met with "all pretty much sound the same."

Brian, summing up Jodi and Kimmy's experience, said, "So you guys went into Fruitvale Station and some of you got out alive. Some of you did not." Gross. Really gross. I don't know if Brian has seen *Fruitvale Station* or if he hasn't. But if he has, he should know that Fruitvale Station is a place where unarmed black men get shot in the back by police officers. It's a place where *unarmed black men* don't get out alive. It is NOT white women who do comedy. It's been said that political correctness is killing comedy. In my opinion bad jokes are killing comedy. If you're a white comedian who wants to be current or edgy and you make jokes about race, race-related issues, or people of color, you need to do some work on yourself first. You need to examine your own implicit bias. Otherwise it will show up in your set. And it won't be funny. And when the audience groans, I'll say it is not because we're politically correct, it's because you're an asshole.

Brian later described the conversation online as a talk about performing in front of "urban" audiences, but let's be real. Let's call it what it is, they were talking about black people. What *they* act like, what *they* sound like, what *they* think like. The whole tone of the conversation was "them versus us."

If I had a small child riding along in the car with me, buckled up in the backseat, and I asked them very straightforward, simple questions about what they had just heard like, "Do you think black people are good or bad?" They would say bad. If I asked, "Do you think black people are better than, the same as, or worse than white people?" They would say worse. The meaning behind the message is that black people are not the same as white people. They are, in some ways, different and their differences make them less than. Inferior. This, subconsciously, is the message a child would walk away with. It's the message *I* walked away with.

"You have to come on the show and talk about this," said Brian when I brought it up with him (and, yes, I did bring it up with him). I couldn't ignore it. I was too disappointed. Too hurt. "Come on as a guest when we do our live show," he said. "It'll be great."

Will it though?

I had been a guest on one previous occasion. It was their first live episode. Brian and Jodi had deviated from the norm and did a recording at a theater, in front of an audience, instead of at Brian's or Jodi's apartment. Having listened to every episode, I considered myself a super fan and volunteered to comprise a list of the top ten most memorable moments from season one to announce on their show in front of their audience. But this time, for season two, in addition to doing my top ten list, I would talk specifically about race and how their conversation had affected me. Could I really do it? Could I really sit on stage in front of a predominantly white audience and talk about race? I didn't want to. But I knew I had to. I said yes. I felt like I had no choice. This, of course, wasn't true. I did have a choice. I had three. I could go on the show do the top ten list and talk about the episode that had offended me. I could go on the show do the top ten list and not talk about the episode that offended me. Or, I could not go on at all.

But I knew something had to be said and so I chose to go. It's important for me to remember that. How many people listening to that episode had heard what I heard and laughed or thought nothing of it? I chose to show up, stand up, and speak up. I chose discomfort over comfort. Courage over cowardice. And I was scared. Scared I wouldn't make my point. Scared I would make a fool of myself. Scared I wouldn't be heard. Scared I wouldn't be understood. Scared of the aftermath. Scared of a fallout between friends. Scared. Scared. Scared.

I sat in the audience for forty-five minutes waiting to go on. And then I was invited to join Brian, Jodi, and another guest up on stage. They introduced me first, and then we talked about my deactivating my Facebook account, which I had done the week before, and then we went into the top ten list. Here's how it began:

> Jodi: Melva is, like, our biggest fan and listens to every episode, so this took a lot of time for her to have to go back through and listen to our bullshit from I don't know how many episodes to find ten moments, so we really appreciate your loyalty and your love.
>
> Me: Thank you, thank you.
>
> *Applause, cheers from the audience.*
>
> Me: And you know these moments, this is a list that's comprised of moments that, of course, made me laugh, and I found very entertaining, but also very, like, thought-provoking stuff that—
>
> Jodi: We do that sometimes.
>
> Me: Yeah, you guys raise some good questions. So that being said…Okay…So number ten, I have to start with the episode that for me is kind of the elephant in the room, the episode that you guys had with guest Kimmy Roberts…where you talked about black people for, like, twenty minutes.…
>
> Jodi and Brian: Okay.…
>
> Me: Now, I don't want to make this into a town hall meeting about race, but I just had to mention, as your number one fan, and as a person of color, I'm compelled

to talk about the impact it had on me, because there were a couple of moments that I thought were a little distasteful—

Brian: Do you want to set up what the conversation was? Basically Jodi—

Guest: It was entirely Kimmy's fault, right?

Laughs from the audience.

Brian: So Jodi and Kimmy, that show you did in Oakland you alluded to earlier—

Jodi: We did a gig and it was an all-black audience, and it was just intimidating as a white girl going up in front of an all-black audience and…is that already insulting? Is that already insulting?

Me: No, I just find that ironic because I'm a black girl going up in front of a predominantly white audience right now.

Laughs, applause, cheers from the audience.

Jodi: Right, and that could be intimidating.

Me: I'm not intimidated.

Stop the tape. I was surprised at just how true the words were. I wasn't intimidated. I wasn't scared. I was just me. Someone who had something to say. Any fear I had felt had left my body the moment I took my seat and sat on stage. The audience helped. They were amazing. They laughed when I needed them to laugh and cheered when I needed them to cheer. They were on my side. And so, it seemed, were Brian, Jodi, and their guest. They were receptive at least. I said what I had to say and then we moved on. I talked about my takeaway from the whole thing. How when it came to race and racism there was always a disconnect for me between the kids I used to nanny for and the parents I worked for. How those, I'm sure, were the kinds of conversations that white kids overheard all the time, whether from parents, friends of the family, or whoever. Conversations about race are loaded with implicit racial bias, heavy undertones that give a clear perspective about people of color. Kids pick up on everything. Every. Little. Thing. I remembered the phone call Mom had had with Bethany's mom after the incident in reading circle. "We were having a *conversation* about race and Bethany *misunderstood.*" I always imagined their conversation to be a serious sit-down discussion about race. When, in actuality, it was probably just Bethany's parents mouthing off about some black folks they knew, and Bethany overheard it. Of course, it could have been more sinister than that, but one is just as effective as the other where kids are concerned. White parents are passing on their own implicit racial bias to their children, and they don't even know it. They won't know it until their child sits next to a black kid in reading circle, stands next to them in the lunch line, or runs into them on the school playground. If you don't tell kids the meaning behind a message, they'll make one up on their own.

At the end of the show I mentioned to Brian and Jodi how glad I was that we had a relationship where we could have a conversation about race. I told them that everyone talks about having a conversation about race, but we had actually done it. The audience cheered and applauded again. And Brian and Jodi seemed pleased. The show had gone well, the top ten list had gone well, and everything I brought up about race and racism had resulted in a lively debate in which no one got hurt. I left the theater feeling like I had superpowers. I did what I'd come to do, and I did it well. The people in the audience complimented me and said how much they agreed with everything I had said. A white guy who had been in Oakland with Jodi and Kimmy told me he realized for a moment what it must feel like to be a black person surrounded by white people. Okay, listen, man, my discomfort is not the same as yours. Got it? No, of course not. Even when white people think they get it they don't. Still, I went home that night feeling like the person on that stage is the person I was meant to be.

A day or two later, I received a call from Brian. "Jodi wants to cut the top ten list from the live episode."

"Wait. What?"

"Not all of it. She wants to start at five and make it a top five list."

"Why?" I asked, although I already knew the answer.

"She's afraid she comes across as racist."

Are you kidding me? I was still being censored. I had been so careful, too. I had been careful not to use the word racist. I had been careful to say that we all, no matter what color we are, have implicit bias. I had been careful to stay calm and did not point too many fingers or lay too much blame. I had been careful. And it wasn't enough.

We went back and forth on it. Brian understood where I was coming from and was in favor of keeping the top ten list. He thought the talk went well, but Jodi felt otherwise. What was so alarming to me was that Jodi was more concerned about the episode in which she felt like I was calling her racist than she was about the episode in which she *actually* came across as racist. There was no mention of taking down the previous episode, the one where she went on and on about black people.

"Let me go back and talk to her and see what I can do. I think she just needs some time."

After a few days Brian had sorted it out. When the episode aired, the top ten list was intact. I won. It took a lot out of me, but I won.

The podcast exists now only on Brian's computer. I think my last appearance on the show might have had something to do with that. It made him and Jodi realize that they had been saying things that were problematic, things that they might get called out on later and would be forced to answer to, and so they took all the episodes down. When he learned I was writing about my experience on the podcast and the episode that had hurt me so deeply, he asked that I change his and everyone else's name and not use the name of the podcast in case readers decided to do some digging. He didn't want Kimmy, Jodi, or himself to get "Megyn Kelly-ed," he said later. I understood, I guess, but I was still annoyed.

The purpose of sharing my story is not to shame anyone. And yet we live in a society where Brian, a white guy, and his shame about race and racism is more important than what I, a black woman, and what I experienced, what I suffered, have to say about it. He was kind enough, though, to send me the episode that offended me so that I could listen to it again. When I did, it was just as bad as I remembered except it wasn't twenty minutes long as I had originally thought—it was five. All of that in five minutes. They had offended me in so many ways it had felt as if it went on forever. My misconception of time speaks to my cumulative experience with microaggressions, how layered and multifaceted it is. The comments and jokes in that episode spoke to a deep-rooted pain in me, one that has been mounting since I was six. But what was so remarkable was that, for the first time ever, I answered back to that pain. I didn't just let it sit there and fester. I gave voice to it. That, I had never done before.

THE WOMEN'S MARCH

Growing up, I didn't see the world in terms of boys and girls, men and women. To me it was always black and white. I learned the names of Civil Rights activists, not feminists. Feminism wasn't something I thought about until I was well into adulthood. Perhaps that's because so much of the feminist framework was, and still is, centered on the experiences of white women, not women of color. Our stories were, and continue to be, excluded from the conversation. I know when white women won the right to vote. I know how much money they make compared to white men. Their experience is mainstream. While the experiences of women of color, our trials and triumphs, are pushed to the side. We remain invisible.

I was on a playdate in Malibu, sitting on the beach next to Nora, a fifty-year-old white woman who owned a house a few feet away. Her son and the young girl I was nannying were running in and out of the ocean, riding the waves on boogie boards. They got out of the water and started drawing in the sand—a big heart with my initials and my ex-boyfriend's initials.

Nora, noticing the sand engraving, asked, "How's the boyfriend?"

"We broke up," I said. "The kids don't know. I didn't have the heart to tell them."

The kids admired their work, pointed it out to me, and laughed, echoing my name and that of my ex-boyfriend's in a mock singsong voice, haunting me with the hope of relationships past. After a small snack they returned to the ocean and Nora and I were left alone again. I dreaded those moments. It was my least favorite part of the job—socializing with moms on playdates. But Nora was surprisingly easy to talk to. Perhaps because she didn't stop. Not when it came to men and women and relationships.

She talked for the next hour about how she tried to divorce her husband twice. How she left him and her son one night when he refused to do it himself. How marriage is a business relationship. I listened intently to her every word. She was filled with insight and intrigue. I felt like I was sitting in on a private TED talk custom-made for me. Would it be weird if I started taking notes? By the end of the conversation I felt wiser. I shared this with her, adding that she should travel the country giving lectures to young women. She laughed appreciatively. Nora was my new favorite person on the planet. That is until she concluded the conversation with this: "I don't care what color you are, being a woman is far more difficult than being a man." And a strained silence settled between us. She broke it by adding, "And if you're a woman of color, well, then, that I can't even imagine."

I surrendered a small smile but felt depleted, detached. Here I thought there was a connection between us, that she had spoken to me, seen me. In truth, she hadn't seen me at all. I was listening to a white woman tell me, a black woman, when color has weight and when it does not. Is this what white feminism looks like? Was I seeing it up close? She simultaneously ruled out the reality of racism so long as a man experienced it, while at the same time acknowledging the harshness of racism when a woman experienced it. I felt strangely taken advantage of. I felt like she had lured me into a false sense of security by opening up about her marriage and consoling me about my breakup, so she could minimize the hardships of black and brown men in order to maximize those of white women. I wanted to say, "You don't get to decide when color is significant and when it's not. You don't get to choose the reality of race just to suit your own position, your own argument. You don't get to make that call. If anyone gets to make that call, it's me."

Nora had mistakenly assumed that when it came to struggle, I had more in common with white women than I did with black men. Did she really think that I thought the hardships she had faced in her life rivaled that of my own father's? I guess so. I know she wanted me to side with her, but I couldn't. My experience of living in a black body has always outweighed my experience of living in a female body, and rightly so, because that is the part of me that has always been under attack.

On January 21, 2017, I went to the Women's March in Los Angeles. I arrived in Pershing Square with a few friends. Almost as soon as we joined the march I spotted a woman on the sidewalk with protest posters for people to grab. She had three or four signs. One of the signs said, "Black Lives Matter." Another sign was for women's rights. I hesitated, not knowing which one to take. Black Lives Matter? Or Women's Rights? Which part of me was I fighting for today? Which part of me do I honor? In retrospect, I should have grabbed both and held one in each hand, but at the time that didn't seem like an option. I felt like I was being asked to choose. Race or gender?

I grabbed the Black Lives Matter sign. It spoke to me. The women's rights sign did not. It felt feeble. It was a whisper. The Black Lives Matter sign was a roar. That's the one I wanted. That's the part of me I was fighting for. That's the part of me I wanted to honor. That's the part of me I felt was most threatened by the new administration. My blackness. I marched with the sign for maybe a minute. Then I rolled it up and let it hang by my side. I'd walk a few paces, unroll the sign and hold it back up in the air. I'd march with it for maybe a minute before rolling it back up and letting it hang back by my side. I went back and forth like this throughout the march. Something was off. A heated debate was taking place inside my head. To be seen or not to be seen? Hyper-visibility or invisibility? When I arrived at the march my blackness was invisible, but choosing to carry a Black Lives Matter sign suddenly made my blackness hyper-visible. I became the black girl again. Only this time it was my choice. No one was choosing it for me. Usually someone says something that throws my blackness into the spotlight, but not that day. That day it was up to me. And I couldn't decide. Why was that?

I searched for others who might be carrying the sign as well but only spotted a few. The vast majority had signs about women's rights and the new administration. Somehow my Black Lives Matter sign didn't seem to belong at that march. I felt odd including it. But as I rolled it up and let it hang by my side, I felt more insecure than I had before. More uncomfortable. Like I was keeping a part of myself hidden. I had gone from hyper-visible to invisible in a matter of minutes. And neither one felt right. A young woman approached me holding a camera. She asked if she could take my picture. I told her I'd rather she didn't. I didn't know what the picture was being used for. Plus, I was having a very private moment in a very public space. I felt self-conscious and didn't really want my feeling of discomfort documented by a stranger. She looked disappointed and walked away.

Hyper-visibility makes me uncomfortable. It always has. My experience with it has always been a negative one. And yet, I can slowly feel myself stepping into it. Invisibility no longer suits me. Blending in no longer suits me. I want to be seen. I want my blackness to be bold. But I want it to be on my terms. The microaggressions I experienced as a child, and even still as an adult, taught me to keep my blackness in a box. And so the times in which I choose to break out of that box are still very uncomfortable for me. Today nearly everything I do comes down to hyper-visibility and invisibility. Whether I want my blackness to be seen or heard. It's a struggle every day. Every. Single. Day. The march felt like it was for a part of me but not all of me. I don't think that reflects poorly on the organizers or the march itself, but more so where we are as a nation and where I am on my journey. Knowing what I know now, it seems impossible for me not to have had the experience I'd had at the Women's March. How am I to know when my blackness is acceptable and when it is not? The march was meant to be inclusive. It was meant to bring people together, to honor our differences, so that we may work together toward a common and unifying goal. Suddenly I was being asked to embrace my blackness, when for years I had been told not to. For years, white women have told me that my gender is more valuable than my race. I'm told this every time I hear how much (white) women make compared to (white) men. I'm told this every time I hear when (white) women won the right to vote. I'm told this every time I hear a statistic about the white woman's experience. How could I allow my blackness to be a part of the march when it had never been part of the conversation? How many of the white women marching believed, as Nora had, that no matter what color you are, being a woman was far more difficult than being a man? How many of the white women who marched that day stayed silent about Sandra Bland, Renisha McBride, or Marissa Alexander? How many of the white women who marched that day are now "taking a knee" during the national anthem? What about the fact that Miss Texas, a white woman, could call out the forty-fifth president on his anemic response to white supremacists and neo-Nazis marching in Charlottesville, Virginia, but a black sports journalist on ESPN could not do the same without her job being threatened. There is a disconnect between white women and black women. I feel that disconnect in my body, in my bones. It affects how I moved through the march that day, and it affects how I move through the world.

I'M GOING TO PRETEND YOU DIDN'T JUST SAY THAT

I've been called a nigger once and a racist twice, but to be fair, I'm pretty sure the man who called me a nigger was on drugs, and my friend who called me a racist was going through a breakup, so neither he nor she was in a good place. The man was dirty. He was walking funny and his eyes were all bugged out. I was crossing La Cienega Boulevard in West Hollywood, and as we passed each other I heard him mumble something like, "Everyone hold on to your stuff there's a nigger coming." I turned my head, wondering if I had heard him correctly, and then I continued along the crosswalk, breathing in and out, one foot in front of the other, like nothing had happened.

The first time Amy called me a racist, we were sitting in a restaurant discussing the comedy show we had just seen, who and what we liked, who and what we didn't like. "I didn't like that black guy," I said.

Amy's eyes grew wide. "*Whoa*. You didn't like *that* black guy?" she repeated in disbelief. "You're a racist."

I hear white people call other white people racist all the time. It's a joke to them. I heard Amy call a friend of ours a racist and he laughed it off, unbothered by it. I heard that same friend do the same thing to someone else as if it was no big deal. But to someone who has actually experienced racism it *is* a big deal. It isn't something I take lightly. In that moment, I felt like Amy was treating me like I was one of her white friends. She didn't see me or my blackness. I know this because if she had seen me for the fullness of who I am, my blackness and all, she wouldn't have called me a racist. She would have known better.

The second time Amy called me a racist, I was at her house having lunch with her and one of her friends. I had gotten the name of the guy she had just stopped dating wrong. He was Latino and had a popular Latino name but I had called him by another popular Latino name by mistake. "Racist," she said. Amy's friend looked away and didn't saying anything. My whole body tensed up. It was worse the second time around, because she'd said it in front of her friend, another white person to witness it. I was embarrassed and angry at both myself and Amy, because I had convinced myself that Amy had known she'd made a mistake the first time, that it had somehow dawned on her and she was really sorry about it. But I had been wrong. She hadn't learned anything. It amazes me the stories I tell myself in order to survive.

Throughout lunch I was mouthing off inside my head. *Identifying someone by their race isn't racist, calling someone by the wrong name isn't racist. I think I know a little bit more about racism than you. You haven't experienced a day of racism in your life. If you want to call out racism, figure out what it is first. If you can't figure it out, ask me—I know. Don't try to tell me what racism is or isn't. That's not your job.* It was yet another subtle form of superiority. Her *idea* of racism outweighed my *experience* of racism. White people, here's a tip. The next time you want to tell a black person about racism try listening instead.

Cognitive Dissonance. Like microaggression, the term beautifully breaks down my experience as a black woman in white America. (I love any word that can do that.) For a long time I didn't even know words like microaggression and cognitive dissonance existed. They weren't part of my vocabulary, and now that they are, my experience in white America doesn't feel as nameless or invisible as it did before. And that is a powerful thing.

According to the app on my phone, cognitive dissonance is anxiety that results from simultaneously holding contradictory or otherwise incompatible attitudes, beliefs, or the like, such as when one likes a person but disapproves strongly of one of his or her habits. *Ding, ding, ding.* It's the shit I go through every day with white people. White people I work for, white people I work with, white people I like, white people I love, white people who have been in my life for over half my life.

In truth, I experience cognitive dissonance with most of my friends. For the past year or two or three—I've lost count—I've listened to my friend Brian, the comedy writer whose podcast I was a guest on, complain about not being able to get staffed on a TV show because of who he is—a middle-class, gay white man. According to Brian, each of those words worked against him. White men get staffed on shows every year. They make up the majority of those positions; however, in recent years, there has been a push to hire more women and people of color. Brian has the attitude that someone else is taking what's his. I mostly listen, because unless I have a supportive word to say, it's hard to get a word in at all. As I listen, there's a voice inside my head that wants to say, *Stop, just stop. I am not the one to wipe away your white tears. That job belongs to somebody else.* As a black woman, I don't want to hear a white man complain about how he thinks he's being discriminated against. I have absolutely no interest in listening to it, but he's my friend, and I love him, so I do.

When Bill Maher said the *N* word on his show, Brian defended him. We were at dinner with Amy when the conversation came up. One of Brian's lines of defense was that Maher had said the word with an "a" and not an "er." *Are you kidding me right now?* This is my friend. This is my very close, very dear friend. I couldn't believe what I was hearing. Somehow I resisted the urge to get up and walk away. Instead I fought back. But Brian fought harder. He always fights harder. We talked about Ice Cube's rebuttal when he was a guest on Maher's show the following week. Brian called Ice Cube angry.

Amy was a great ally. "I agree with you ninety percent of the time, Brian, but not on this," she said and pointed out how he needed to watch the language he used when describing black men. Just because Ice Cube (or Ice-T, as Amy and Brian kept calling him by mistake) took issue with what Maher had said didn't make him "angry."

"Oh, so black people can't be angry now?" Brian said.

I didn't talk to him for three months after that night, but I don't think he noticed. In Los Angeles, it's hard to know if a friend is mad at you or if they just don't want to deal with the traffic. Three months can easily go by without two close friends seeing or speaking to each other—it's no big deal.

Almost a year later, Brian and I were on the phone talking about Roseanne Barr being fired after her racist tweet about former Obama advisor Valerie Jarrett. Brian wasn't defending what Roseanne said—not exactly. However, he did say he didn't think she was a racist. He had said that when it came to Roseanne he thought he had cognitive dissonance, and all I could think was, *I have cognitive dissonance when it comes to you.*

"Do you have cognitive dissonance when it comes to me?" Amy asked. She and I were out having dinner and drinks. Just the two of us. It was Wine Wednesday at Mess Hall in Los Feliz. Half off bottles. We ordered one to split. I had just finished telling her about my conversation with Brian. I hesitated. "You can tell me," she said. "Do you?"

The truth was I did. I had been waiting to have the conversation with her for a long time and the moment had finally come. I didn't want to say anything, but I knew I had to. I needed to. I took a deep breath and began. I told her about the night we were at a bar and talking about dating and getting married one day, and I had mentioned how black women were the population group least likely to marry. She had said, "Isn't it part of the culture?"

Now, without hesitation she apologized. "I'm so sorry," she said. "I'm so sorry."

No adult has ever apologized to me the way Amy did that night. It was such a deliberate and definitive apology. I didn't know what to do with it. I didn't have to explain to her why it was wrong, why it was offensive, or why it hurt me. She knew. She understood. She got it. Immediately. "I'm so sorry. I'm so sorry." Another moment passed, and she said it again. "I'm so sorry. I am so sorry." She said it over and over. She said she couldn't believe she would say such a thing. She had no recollection of saying it at all. It's no wonder, I thought, it didn't impact her the way it had me. She continued to apologize. I thanked her but the apologies kept coming. She was sorry that I had been carrying this with me for all these years, that it must have really hurt to hold on to it for so long. She teared up. I think a part of me had been expecting this and I wasn't sure how to handle it. I knew it wasn't *my* responsibility to comfort *her* for saying something racially insensitive to *me*, but at the same time it was hard to look into the face of a friend who was hurting and not do anything.

"Obviously I know that you're a good, well-intentioned person. I don't want *you* to carry this around with you now," I said.

"Nope," she said. "Don't worry about me. I'm an adult." She wasn't going to let me comfort her. She wasn't going to let her own hurt outweigh the hurt she had caused, and I was grateful. Shocked and grateful. "I wish I met you now," she said. "I'm so much more aware now than when we first met."

It made me sad to hear it. "Don't say that," I said. "If we met now, we would have missed out on so many fun times. Going to Vegas. Going to Joshua Tree."

She smiled. "Joshua Tree was fun," she said. She told me how I was her only black friend when we met and that was no longer the case. A part of me was, like, who are these other black friends of yours and why haven't I met them? But I let it go. There were other things to talk about. I moved on to the two times she called me a racist. "It's just a bit jarring," I said, "as a black woman, to be called a racist by someone who hasn't experienced racism a day in her life."

"I'm sure I was just joking," she said. "I probably thought I was being cool. But, yeah, I can see, though, how you must have been like, fuck you."

Ding, ding, ding!

She got it. And that's all I could ask for. That she get it. Really get it. And she did. I told her what my therapist had told me. Racism is prejudice plus power. She repeated the words. Prejudice plus power.

"I'm going to hold on to that," she said.

I jumped back to the first incident. There was something I left out and I wanted to make sure I got everything on the table. You also said, "Don't grandmothers sometimes raise their grandchildren?" I told her I wasn't sure what she meant by it. Lastly, I told her how she had told me that I might have to marry outside my race. I was just trying to connect the dots, I told her. I still am. *Isn't it part of the culture? Don't grandmothers sometimes raise their grandchildren? You might have to marry outside your race.* What did it all mean? Where was it coming from? What was she trying to say?

"I don't think I was in a very good place," she said.

I returned to the incident of her calling me a racist. "It seemed like more of a projection," I said. I told her how I'd heard white people call each other racist. How it seemed as if they were so afraid to be called racist themselves they were trying to beat each other to it. And how disconcerting it was to hear the word racist being used casually without consequence, while when a black person used it with sincerity there was so much backlash. She nodded her head and apologized again. "You've also been a good ally," I added. "Remember that time we were at that bar sitting in a booth and that white guy slid in to sit with us and then started asking me about O.J. Simpson?"

"You're being very gracious to me," she said.

"I just feel it's only fair to mention that, too," I said.

It had been a Sunday night. Amy had just said, "If we were in New York a guy would have offered to buy us drinks by now." And then, as if on cue, a white guy with spiky blond hair slid into our booth and started talking as though the three of us had already met. He was in his early twenties. I know this because he had said twenty-five was repulsive to him, and Amy and I had broken out into laughter. He never introduced himself nor did he say hello. He acted as though he'd excused himself mid-conversation to go to the restroom or buy a drink and had returned ready to pick up where we had left off.

"So, the O.J. Simpson trial…what were your thoughts?"

"Excuse me…?"

"What were your thoughts? On the O.J. Simpson trial?"

"You mean from, like, fifteen years ago?"

Amy and I stared blankly at one another but the dude with spiky blond hair had eyes only for me. When I didn't give him anything to go on about the O.J. Simpson trial, he went on to talk about a fight that had broken out at his school after a basketball game. He seemed to want my thoughts on that too. I gathered the fight was race-related. Just a hunch.

"I'm sorry, but…" began Amy, and then thinking better of it, stopped herself. "No, never mind," she said.

I cut in, having a sense of what she might say. "No, say it," I said.

"Okay," she said, turning to the dude with spiky blond hair. "I feel like you only came over here to talk to us because Melva's black."

Thank you.

Thank you.

Thank you.

That was what being an ally looked like. Using your voice so I don't have to use mine. The dude with spiky blond hair was offended that she would suggest such a thing and then a friend of his came over to our booth to check on him. It was at that point I took off my cardigan, feeling a bit warm, and the dude with spiky blond hair looked at me and said, "Madam, please cover your shoulders." His friend took hold of him and steered him away, leaving Amy and me to wonder what had just happened. That was what white privilege looked like. Stepping into someone's space without fear, without apology, and expecting them to answer to you. Imagine me sitting down at *his* table, expecting *him* to answer to *me* about the Birmingham church bombing, Jim Crow, or slavery. Still, Amy had been an incredible ally that night. She and I had been friends for only a short amount of time at that point but I felt like it was the moment that really sealed the deal for us.

I mean, when it comes to race, no one has ever really stood up for me like that. And there at Mess Hall, I started to tear up too.

"You're being very gracious," Amy said again. We sat in silence for a bit, sipping our wine. "I'm going to do better," she said. "I'm going to do the work."

"You know, I never have conversations like this, so I really appreciate you being so open to it."

"You're being very gracious," she said a third time.

"It's true," I said. "I normally hold it in. I usually say nothing."

"I always thought you were a class act," she said. "You just let things roll off your back. I remember when I first met you, I was just, like, Melva has such class."

Out of everything that was shared and said between us

that night, that was the moment I held on to. Her final words to me were all I could think about on my ride home and as I climbed into bed that night. I couldn't help but think how hard I had been on myself throughout the years, how much I had beaten myself up. How I had taken my silence as a sign of weakness. I was so thankful, so appreciative, that Amy had offered me something new, had reframed the way I thought about myself. What I had called cowardice she had called class.

MINORITIES ENCOURAGED TO ATTEND

It wasn't the casting notice that caught my eye but the four words printed in bold below it—Minorities Encouraged To Attend. I never liked the word minority. It sounds like a disability—like someone who's wheeled around by a nurse, spoon-fed Jell-O, or spoken to loudly in one ear. Limited. Less than. Still, my heart leapt despite itself. Minority meant me.

I circled the casting notice and highlighted the four words below it. Seeing those words on a job posting was what I imagine seeing a handicap sign in a parking lot is to those who are in need of one. It meant there was a spot for me— or someone *like* me—but that wasn't entirely true, was it? It was an invitation, really—more like a courtesy invite. It meant I was being asked to show up to a place where I might otherwise feel I didn't belong.

If I have to be encouraged, it has to mean that at some point in my life I've been discouraged. I know this, of course, but it's a relief to know that someone else does, too. I think that's why I was holding on to those four words so dearly and studying them so closely. The black experience is so often denied by white America that I find myself challenging my own truth. The voice of the opposition is so loud inside my head that it drowns out my very own thoughts. I therefore look for and grasp onto the slightest suggestion that my experience exists outside myself. Minorities Encouraged To Attend is the validation that my experience is real. It's not a promise of employment, as some might believe it to be, it's proof that I exist—we exist.

How, then, do we deal with daily doses of discouragement?

The most immediate work, the most pressing work, the most challenging work, I think, is the work we do on ourselves. Because the moment we start to believe their words to be true, we're lost. The moment we start to accept their image of us as our own, we're lost.

I see black women every day who are my age, who grew up in the city, who grew up in the suburbs, who speak truth to power, who raise their fists, who answer back to bias, who answer back to bigotry, who strut their shit, who give zero fucks. And I'm like, how can I get in on that? I'd like to say I give zero fucks but it's far from true. I've got a shitload. A shitload of miscellaneous fucks to pass out at my discretion. And I'm ticking them off, one by one. One for you, and you, and you. One day I'll run out. One day I'll reach into my big bag of fucks and realize I have none left. But today is not that day. Today I'm still negotiating with the world I live in. Narrowing the gap between who I am and who I strive to be. I look at today's youth. I see their confidence, their courage. And I think, I wish I had that. I wish I'd grown up with that. I think of all the little black girls and little black boys in cities and suburbs, and I wonder if they're receiving the message we, the black community, are sending. Is it reaching them? And if it is, what are they going to do next?

I've never wanted to be anyone other than who I am. Never. In fact, being told I'm not black enough, I realize, is just another part of the black experience. It doesn't strip me of who I am. It reaffirms who I am. In truth, the only time I've felt ashamed were the moments I didn't stand up for myself. And the moments I felt most proud were the moments I stood up for others. So that's what I'm going to do.

Show up.

Stand up.

Speak up.

If the black community hadn't shown up for themselves

we'd still be sitting at the back of the bus, coming home to crosses burning on our lawns and to nooses hanging from our trees. The life I'm living today is solely because black people before me showed up. And I'm grateful for that. I thank God for that. So why, then, am I so hesitant to do so now? Perhaps it's because I know what happens when you show up as you are. I've known it since I was six years old when I sat next to my friend in reading circle. I knew it in sixth grade when I sat on stage with my classmates and was singled out for having dark skin. I knew it in high school when I was told I wasn't black enough. I've known it as an actress limited by labels, given notes based on my color and not on my portrayal of the character. And I know it now as a part-time activist working my way to a full-time position. When we show up as we are, we're shamed for it. And that shame leads to silence. Or so it has for me. And when we're silenced, we stop showing up for ourselves. And when we stop showing up for ourselves, we can't thrive. We can't survive.

As society evolves so, too, does racism. The racism my parents and grandparents grew up with is not the racism I grew up with. Instead of a mighty sword it became a subtle knife. Today we live with both, one in each hand. Microaggressions on the left. Macroaggressions on the right. They are both part of the black experience, black American life. But the struggle looks different on everyone. My story is what it looks like on me.

I can't speak for the entire black community. I can only speak for myself. And even that I'm reluctant to do. Silence means safety. If I'm not seen and I'm not heard, I can't be hurt. But the suffering doesn't stop. The struggle doesn't end. It swells until it becomes unbearable, and you're fighting from the inside out. I know that now. The current racial climate is a catastrophic storm, and silence is a shitty shield.

Therefore, minorities, I encourage you to attend. I encourage you to show up. I encourage you to stand up. I encourage you to speak up. I encourage you to hold on to who you are. I encourage you to celebrate who you are. I encourage you to rejoice in who you are. I encourage you to encourage others. Yes, please, please, please encourage others. I encourage you to take a deep breath. I encourage you to curl up in bed. And I encourage you to set your alarm so that you get back up.

I encourage you.

I encourage you.

I encourage you.

Showing up for yourself, showing up for others, is what activism really is, but it looks different on everyone. Know that. Respect that. Find out what it looks like on you and then commit yourself to it.

But, believe me, I'll understand if you don't.

I'll understand if you need to sit this one out. If you decide to stay on the sidelines because it feels safe and right now you just need to feel safe. I'll understand if it's too scary to speak your own name, let alone your own mind. I'll understand if you hide under your dining room table. Really, I get it. Know, please know, that is okay too—you'll get there when you get there. And when you do you won't be alone, you'll have me, and maybe, when you see me, you'll see yourself and be encouraged.

ACKNOWLEDGMENTS

If I kept a gratitude journal, which I will surely start any day now, a long list of allies, advocates, friends, and family members would be in it. Mom and Dad, Micah and Andrew, Aunt Tootsie, Aunt Faye and Uncle Lynn, I am so very appreciative of all that you've done and continue to do for me. Thank you for having my back and being in my corner. Thank you for the love and support you have shown me throughout my life and this entire process. Thank you Jennifer Hayes for your compassion over the past several years and being kind to me when I wasn't always kind to myself. Thank you Brooke Barber Kostelnik, Leslie Marseglia, Gary Patent, Derrick Abrenica, Demetrius Butler, Tom Patterson, Anna Carey, Jason Romaine, Nicholas Gorham, Asher Bailey, and Emily Bunce for long talks and pep talks, reading my work, giving me feedback, inviting me over, and calling me back. As Sara Crewe tells her friends in *A Little Princess*, after they've stolen her locket back from Miss Minchin, "You all are the best friends anyone could ever ask for."[1] I'd like to thank editor-in-chief Jaynie Royal, senior editor Pam Van Dyk, and the entire team at Regal House Publishing for believing in my book and bringing it to life. I'd also like to thank my agent Andrea Somberg for hearing what I had to say and making sure others heard it too.

I am deeply indebted to each of you.

Thank you.

---

[1] LaGravenese Richard, Elizabeth Chandler, and Liesel Matthews. *A Little Princess*. Amazon Prime video streaming service. Directed by Alfonso Cuarón. Burbank, CA: Warner Bros. Pictures, 1995.